A MIRROR OF CHAUCER'S WORLD

PRINCETON UNIVERSITY PRESS
PRINCETON, NEW JERSEY

A Mirror of Chaucer's World

BY ROGER SHERMAN LOOMIS

Yit somme holden oppynyon and sey
That none ymages schuld imaked be.
Thei erren foule and goon out of the wey
Of trouth; have thei scant sensibilite.

THOMAS HOCCLEVE, Regement of Princes

L.C. Card 65-10830
ISBN 0-691-01349-7 (paperback edition)
ISBN 0-691-06079-7 (hardcover edition)

ROGER SHERMAN LOOMIS: B.A., D.Litt., Williams;
M.A., Harvard; B.Litt., M.A., Oxon.; D.Litt., Wales;
Docteur Honoris Causa, Rennes; D.Litt., Columbia
(Professor Emeritus, Columbia, 1956).
Professor Loomis, Fellow of the Mediaeval Academy,
won the Academy's Haskins Medal in 1951. He was President
of the American Branch of the International
Arthurian Society, 1948-1963.

AUTHOR OF

Arthurian Tradition and Chrétien de Troyes (Columbia)
Wales and the Arthurian Legend (Wales)
The Grail: From Celtic Myth to Christian Symbol (Columbia)
The Development of Arthurian Romance (Hutchinson)

EDITOR OF

Arthurian Literature in the Middle Ages (Clarendon)

TRANSLATOR OF

The Romance of Tristram and Ysolt, by
Thomas of Britain (Columbia)

*

Fourth hardcover printing, 1978
First PRINCETON PAPERBACK printing, 1978

Printed in the United States of America
by The Meriden Gravure Company, Meriden, Connecticut

Amicae Uxorique Carae

Dorotheae Bethurum Loomis

PREFACE

IN THE COURSE of my researches and of assembling the illustrative material for this book, I have incurred a considerable debt to individuals and institutions on both sides of the Atlantic. First, let me mention, however, the professors who introduced me to Chaucer before any such project entered my head, namely Byron Johnson Rees of Williams College and Fred Norris Robinson of Harvard University. The latter has increased my obligation of 1909–1910 by his edition of Chaucer's text in 1957, which the publishers, Houghton Mifflin Company, have graciously permitted me to use as the basis of my quotations. Both my teachers of Chaucer have been, happily, my friends as well. Little did I think as I sat in their classrooms that I should one day have the privilege of rendering Chaucer's works, not more intelligible, but more readily and accurately perceptible by the imagination.

Since I assumed that task more than twenty years ago, I have been favored with the friendly assistance of several experts, and, in case I seem to indicate by the order in which I name them a certain gradation, let me adopt that of the alphabet, which is neutral: Miss Mary D. Anderson, author of *Drama and Imagery in English Medieval Churches;* H. S. Bennett of Emanuel College, Cambridge, author of *Chaucer and the Fifteenth Century;* Professor Muriel Bowden of Hunter College, author of *A Commentary on the General Prologue of the "Canterbury Tales";* the late Carleton Brown, successively Secretary and President of the Modern Language Association of America; John H. Harvey, author of *Gothic England* and *Henry Yevele;* W. C. Hassall of the Bodleian Library; Professor Clair C. Olson of the College of the Pacific; Dr. David J. A. Ross of Birkbeck College, author of *Alexander Historiatus;* the late Dr. F. Saxl of the Warburg Institute; Professor Frederick Sternfeld of Oxford University; the late Mrs. W. M. Thoseby, Steward of the Friends of Canterbury Cathedral; Dr. J. B. Trapp of the Warburg Institute; and Professor George Zarnecki of the Courtauld Institute of Art.

Two libraries stand out as sources of manuscript material, the British Museum and the Bibliothèque Nationale. Here let me record my gratitude for forty years of gracious hospitality. I have drawn also on the riches of the Bodleian Library, the Cambridge University Library, the Morgan Library, the Bibliothèque Royale, Brussels, the Huntington Library, the Bibliothèque de l'Arsénal, the University of Aberdeen Library, and the Library of Corpus Christi College, Cambridge; and to the staffs of these institutions I gladly express my thanks. The Society of Antiquaries and the National Buildings Record have rendered invaluable assistance and provided me with photographs not otherwise obtainable. Mr. P. J. Conkwright and Mrs. Jean Lilly of the Princeton University Press contributed their expert knowledge to the preparation of the material for publication. Finally, without the great resources of the Avery and Butler Libraries of my own university, Columbia, and without the cooperative attitude of their staffs, this work would never have been finished.

ROGER SHERMAN LOOMIS

ACKNOWLEDGMENTS

The institutions and individuals listed below have
kindly given permission to reproduce the following figures:

Biblioteca Nazionale, Florence: 69, 70
Bibliothèque de l'Arsénal, Paris: 146, 149
Bibliothèque Nationale, Paris: 9, 10, 12, 44, 45,
46, 47, 48, 52, 58, 60, 61, 64, 65, 67, 72, 73, 103,
119, 120, 123, 124, 130, 131, 137, 139, 140, 144,
147, 151–160, 165, 166
Bibliothèque Royale, Brussels: 43, 127, 142, 171
Bodleian Library, Oxford: 4, 56, 57, 78, 114, 118,
121, 122, 132, 150, 163, 164, 170, 173
British Museum, London: 2, 3, 17, 20, 23, 25, 27,
28, 35, 42, 59, 66, 77, 104, 105, 107, 108, 113,
115, 116, 126, 138, 142, 145, 148, 167, 175
Burrell Collection, Glasgow Art Gallery: 63
Cambridge University Library: 177, 178, 179
Columbia University Library: 109
Corpus Christi College Library, Cambridge: 68

Courtauld Institute of Art, London: 8, 17, 23, 26,
168, 174
Mrs. F. H. Crossley, Chester: 8
Fitzwilliam Museum, Cambridge: 51, 129
Fogg Art Museum, Harvard University: 5
P. M. Goodchild, King's Lynn: 34, 41
Guildhall Museum, London: 106
H. M. Stationery Office, London: 14, 15, 16, 32
Huntington Library, San Marino, California: 1,
80–101
The Masters of the Bench of the Inner Temple,
London: 31
Metropolitan Museum of Art, New York: 71
National Buildings Record, London: 21, 29
National Gallery, London: 22
National Library of Scotland, Edinburgh: 135
Pierpont Morgan Library, New York: 7, 125, 169
Society of Antiquaries, London: 13, 26
University of Aberdeen Library: 49, 50
Victoria and Albert Museum, London: 36

CONTENTS

INTRODUCTION

FRANCIS BEAUMONT, father of the dramatist, made the following critical comment on the poet Chaucer: "One gift he hath above all other authors, and that is by the excellence of his descriptions to possess his readers with a stronger imagination of seeing that done before their eyes, which they read, than any other that ever writ in any tongue."

Not everyone will agree with this extreme claim for Chaucer's descriptive powers; there are other strong contenders for the prize. But few will deny what is implicit in Beaumont's comment, that one of the chief pleasures of reading a poem or a novel resides in the vividness and the clarity of the images evoked. And there can be little doubt that this is an effect which the author seeks.

Why else did Chaucer recall the Prioress's demure smile, or her brooch with its ambiguous inscription, "Amor vincit omnia," unless he meant us to see them? Why did he describe in such detail the House of Fame, or the physical beauty of the Duchess Blanche? Was it merely to display a copiousness of invention, a rich vocabulary, and a virtuosity in riming? Surely, rather, the poet hoped to stir the reader's imagination and induce in some degree the pleasure which he himself felt in visualizing people, places, and things.

It was easy enough for Chaucer's friends who listened to his recitation or read his lines to see what he saw with the mind's eye. But six centuries, more or less, have passed since he penned his descriptions of the Knight and the Pardoner, Alice of Bath and Alisoun of Oxford, the Garden of the Rose and the Temple of Mars. The world and its people have changed their outer aspect enormously. Many words and things have become obsolete. What is a *taille*, a *mazelyn*, a *bracer*, a *giterne?* Even when one has consulted a glossary, the resultant image is likely to be vague. Worse still, the image evoked can be quite wrong, since our impressions of the Middle Ages are likely to be made up of a jumble of Howard Pyle's drawings of the knights of the Round Table and their ladies, of Christmas card depictions of yuletide festivities, of saints and sinners portrayed by artists of the Italian Renaissance, and perhaps of costumed tenors and prima donnas rendering the *Ring of the Nibelungs* and the *Meistersinger*.

To be sure, some admirers of the poet are satisfied with their own imaginings, regardless of fidelity to the poet's own conceptions. Anachronisms do not worry them, and they do not care whether a *symphonye* is an orchestra, a banjo, or a hurdy-gurdy, so long as it makes a noise; and having learned from a glossary that a *gypon* is a tunic, and a *habergeoun* is a coat of mail, they are content to envisage the *habergeoun* covering the *gypon* and reaching to the ankles or at least the knees! On the other hand, the names of Diana, Orpheus, Hector, and Aristotle recall to them all too vividly Grecian sculptures or painted amphorae such as Chaucer never saw and could not have imagined. He, like his contemporaries, pictured Troy and Rome as medieval towns, and Greeks, Trojans, and Romans as medieval men and women. Most of his modern readers, I suspect, reverse the anachronism by recalling the lion gate at Mycenae and the frieze of the Parthenon.

But not all readers are of so casual a type, so indifferent to the historical setting of the *Canterbury Tales, Troilus and Criseyde,* and the minor poems, so incurious as to the visual aspects of Chaucer's art. There must be a goodly multitude of amateurs and students who, owing to a bump of curiosity, a feeling for accuracy, or a love of the poet, would like to enter his world and see, if not with his eyes, at least with the eyes of a contemporary. They would think it as ridiculous to visualize the fourteenth-century scene through fifteenth- or sixteenth-century spectacles as to illustrate a Victorian novel with the aid of fashion plates and photographs of the year 1965.

Such readers have had hitherto little assistance from editors, commentators, and publishers. Jusserand, Manly, Coulton, Carleton Brown, Dr. Kenneth Sisam, Professor J. A. W. Bennett, and Professor Dorothy Bethurum have each helped by providing illustrative material, but only in a limited way and in widely scattered publications. Spielmann reproduced and discussed the portraits of Chaucer, and the Pilgrims as depicted in the Ellesmere manuscript are familiar. Professor D. W. Robertson has provided liberally from the whole range of the Middle Ages illustrations of the poet's ideological universe, though little that bears directly on the text. Other attempts to bring Chaucer and his work to life through visual media are open to criticism. To quote the late George Sarton: "Some historians will take considerable pains to insure the accuracy of each and every statement and then select relevant or irrelevant illustration with the utmost laxity. . . . Iconographical documents are very important and very impressive, but only if they are genuine and relevant. Considering the easy and cheap means of reproduction available today, no biography or monograph on almost any subject of the history of science should be deemed complete without illustrations which tell in a different way another part of the story and which literally illuminate it."

If these statements hold good for the historian of science, they apply as much or even more to the historian and interpreter of literature. They apply to the illustrator of Chaucer, but not infrequently even he commits gross anachronisms. We are shown the Tabard Inn not as it was in Harry Bailey's time, but as it was rebuilt in the sixteenth century; or a tournament in which the participants are completely accoutered in plate armor. Of course, contemporaneity need not be required of every illustration. Some things alter slowly, if at all. In the fourteenth and fifteenth century, whereas civil costume in high society changed almost as fast as it does today, the robes of priests, bishops, monks, friars, and nuns remained fairly unchanged. Still the aim of the collector of illustrations to Chaucer is to reproduce as far as possible the world as he saw it, his friends, associates, and acquaintances as he knew them, and the stories as he, or at least as his contemporaries, imagined them.

Such a collection is not easy to make. Except for three manuscripts (two of them fragmentary) which depict pilgrims on horseback, another which shows Chaucer reciting *Troilus* to an audience of courtiers, and certain manuscripts of the *Treatise on the Astrolabe* containing diagrams, there are almost no direct illustrations of his work until Caxton's edition. Indeed, perhaps because of visitations of the plague and the effects of the French war, very few handsome manuscripts were produced in England in Chaucer's lifetime, and the few were service books which offer little to illuminate the *Canterbury Tales,* the *House of Fame,* or even the *Legend of Good Women.* English alabaster sculptures, though rather plentiful, are likewise restricted either to religious subjects or to monumental effigies. In England the walls of palaces, castles, and manor houses, which surely in the Middle Ages were adorned with secular paintings, have been stripped of their plaster or whitewashed over, with hardly an exception. It is unnecessary to add that illustrative material in the form of precious metals, fragile textiles, wood and glass, etc., has a very low survival rate.

Working intermittently at the task over the past twenty years or so, searching in the obvious books, visiting the libraries, museums, and medieval buildings of Europe, I have done my best to provide a pictorial companion to Chaucer. With what success it is for others to judge, but I do not believe that there is much suitable material which I have overlooked. Besides the well-known Ellesmere manuscript with its miniatures of the Pilgrims, and the beautiful *Troilus* frontispiece, mentioned above, most precious is the so-called Auchinleck manuscript which Chaucer must once have read with amusement and which inspired that masterpiece of parody, *Sir Thopas;* and valuable, too, is a book of benefactors of St. Albans Abbey with its authentic portrayals of John of Gaunt, Princess Joan of Kent, and Sir John Philipot—all three closely associated with the poet. Then there is the exquisite painting known as the Wilton Diptych, which shows us not only to what delicacy of line and color and feeling an English artist could attain, but also reveals the physical charm of King Richard II, as he is presented by his patron saints to the Madonna. There are the royal monuments in Westminster Abbey and the magnificent effigy of the Black Prince at Canterbury, recalling personages who once loomed large in Chaucer's world. Still impressive as in his time are Westminster Hall and Chapter House, so familiar to him; and we possess pictures (though late) of Windsor Castle and Rochester Bridge much as he knew them. Though no presentation of the Tabard of Harry Bailey's day is known, we are able to reproduce a print of the inn at Canterbury to which, according to a fifteenth-century poem, he conducted the Pilgrims. Superb examples of the metalworker's and enameler's craft are the King's Lynn goblet, the bishop's crozier at New College, Oxford, and the royal gold cup in the British Museum.

The last mentioned is of French workmanship, and French art of the fourteenth century fills in many of the blanks in the English pictorial record. To a student of technique and style there are, of course, noticeable differences between the arts of the two countries, but for our purposes they have little importance, so steeped was Chaucer in French culture, so similar were fashions in Great Britain and the adjacent Continent. French manuscripts illustrate the story of Ceyx and Alcione, some of the tales in the *Legend of Good Women,* and some of the Monk's "tragedyes." They depict Apollo and the Muses, and the winged steed Pegasus, as envisaged by contemporaries of Chaucer. A French drama on the subject of Griselda, dated 1395, supplies a complete set of illustrations for the Clerk's Tale. The *Très Riches Heures* of the Duc de Berry represents the zodiacal scheme for April, to which Chaucer refers in the opening lines of the General Prologue. The manuscripts in which he read the *Roman de la Rose* or the poems of Machaut, Froissart, and Deschamps must have contained miniatures not too different from those which we see today in the Bibliothèque Nationale, and some of which we reproduce. The ateliers of the Low Countries, of Maestricht and Bruges, displayed a fondness for filling the lower margins with genre scenes, irrelevant to the text, but sometimes relevant to the *Canterbury Tales,* for instance, marriage at the church door, and a henwife pursuing a fox. With slight allowances for differences in costume, miniatures in an Italian manuscript of *Il Filostrato,* such as Chaucer may have pored over, may serve to illustrate Chaucer's retelling in *Troilus.* A combination of English, Flemish, and Italian manuscripts provides visual details for the Pardoner's Tale.

In the medium of mural painting France luckily preserves much more than England, and furnishes a portrait of Isoude and a vivid evocation of the monster Chicheface (Chaucer's Chichevache). France has bequeathed to us also a superb tapestry dipicting a medieval Hector.

It may be seen that the collection I have made ranges over wide areas of medieval life, and I venture to claim that there are few corners into which I have not carried my search. As a consequence, I trust that this book will prove of interest not only to lovers of medieval literature, but also to students of the arts and crafts and to social historians. To render these pictorial documents of more value to all concerned I have provided for each one not only indications of its relevance to Chaucer's life or work but also, as far as possible, information as to its location, its date and place of execution, and references to books and periodicals where further information may be found. When the picture requires elucidation, it has been attempted in brief compass.

No book of this kind can escape criticism, and I take this opportunity to anticipate and, so far as I can, to answer some of the objections.

First, it may be said, and truly said, that many of the illustrations do not perfectly represent what Chaucer described, and some actually misrepresent it. Let it be granted at once that this is not the book we might have had if an artist, competent in many styles, working under the poet's own direction, had profusely illustrated his works. Since this desideratum is forever denied us, we have no choice but to take the next best thing—a collection of pictorial material from contemporary sources. Where the image differs from Chaucer's description, as it not infrequently does, we can always make the imaginative correction.

Secondly, critics may justly observe that not all the sources are contemporary, that, in fact, a considerable number belong to the fifteenth century or later. Thus one of the basic principles for the selection of material is violated, and to this extent users of the book may be misled. Several replies to this criticism may be made. The legend accompanying every illustration indicates its precise or approximate date, and no one need be deceived. Most of the fifteenth-century illustrations, including the Ellesmere miniatures, were executed in the first decade when little change had taken place since Chaucer's death, and to exclude these miniatures and the *Troilus* frontispiece would be a *reductio ad absurdum* of the principle of contemporaneity. Even when the gap between Chaucer's day and the illustration is wider, even much wider, as with the stained-glass panel showing Henry II doing penance before the shrine of Becket, or the view of London in 1547, these exceptions to the rule of contemporaneity can be justified. A king, clad in crown and breechcloth, does not look very different, whether portrayed in the twelfth or the fifteenth century; and Becket's shrine, the principal goal of the pilgrimage, was not subject to changes·of fashion. The landmarks of Chaucer's London—the Tower, the Bridge, St. Paul's, Charing Cross—were little affected by the coming of the Tudors and the Reformation, at least in their exterior aspect. Even later engravings of the east window of St. Paul's, of Windsor Castle, of the bridge at Rochester over which the Pilgrims rode, of the West Gate of Canterbury, through which they passed, and of the hostelry, the Chequer of the Hope, where we may suppose that they put up, can be defended, since we are thus enabled to see the buildings much as they looked in the poet's day.

A few other exceptions to the rule of contemporaneity may be justified when the application to Chaucer's text is particularly apt. Such is the wall painting which depicts the gruesome dismemberment of Christ's body by those who swear by his limbs, and such is the lovely rood-screen portrait of St. Cecilia, with her garlands combining the lilies of virginity with the roses of martyrdom.

A certain disproportion in this collection cannot be avoided, namely, that the number of illustrations allotted to a given poem or prose work bears no relation to its importance as a piece of literature. The Clerk's Tale is covered by twelve pictures, whereas *Troilus* has only four, the Prioress's Tale has two, and the Reeve's Tale only one. The tales of the Wife of Bath, the Sergeant of the Law, and the Friar lack illustration entirely. For this, it is not the choices of the collector but the vagaries of chance which are responsible. When suitable illustrative material is scanty or nonexistent, there is nothing to be done but to mourn, with Boethius and his translator, the caprices of Fortune.

Finally, some critics will challenge the inclusion of pictures dealing with subjects of trifling consequence. What does it matter if one cannot form a correct image of a medieval cannon? What could be more irrelevant to the understanding or the enjoyment of the Reeve's Tale than a miniature depicting the Cross of Bromholm, to which the miller's wife appealed when her spouse fell on top of her? Why reproduce the stately effigy of the Black Prince at Canterbury when we have no evidence that he played any significant part in Chaucer's life, and is never mentioned in his work? There is reason in such criticisms, but there are also reasonable answers. If one is to visualize at all, it is better to visualize accurately, and there is no way of picturing Chaucer's *gonne* or the Cross of Bromholm accurately without a picture. As for the Black Prince, there was not in all England a more resplendent figure, and the poet must have had many opportunities of observing him and perhaps conversing with him at Westminster and Windsor. Besides, the effigy is a fine example of English craftsmanship and of knightly equipment.

So with this apologia, but without apologies, I offer this "Mirror of Chaucer's World."

A MIRROR OF CHAUCER'S WORLD

PORTRAITS OF CHAUCER

1. The Ellesmere Portrait

The miniature of the poet on horseback, painted in the margin of the Ellesmere manuscript of the *Canterbury Tales* (Henry E. Huntington Library, San Marino, California) opposite the beginning of *Melibeus,* may well be the earliest extant likeness. J. M. Manly and Edith Rickert date the manuscript 1400–1410, and the "Hoccleve portrait" must be later, since the *Regement of Princes,* to which it is attached, was not begun by Hoccleve till 1411. Indeed, Margaret Rickert believed that the "Hoccleve portrait" might be an adaptation from the Ellesmere miniature, or that both had a common lost prototype. See *Text of the Canterbury Tales,* ed. J. M. Manly and E. Rickert (Chicago, 1940), I, 148, 587–90. Here Chaucer looks somewhat younger than in the other miniature, his hair and beard being yellow rather than white. As to rotundity of figure it confirms his own references and the other portraits. But he was no dwarf, and the shortness of his legs was imposed on the miniaturist by the requirements of the marginal space. Hung from his neck is a case containing an implement, a pen or a *pointel* (a stylus for writing on waxed tablets)—presumably a token of his craft as a writer. On this miniature see E. F. Piper in *Philological Quarterly,* III (1924), 249–52. On all the portraits see M. H. Spielmann, *Portraits of Geoffrey Chaucer* (Chaucer Society, 1900), and A. Brusendorff, *Chaucer Tradition* (London, Copenhagen, 1925), pp. 13–47.

1

2. The "Hoccleve Portrait"

A miniature in MS British Museum Harley 4866, fol. 88. There are three manuscripts containing Thomas Hoccleve's *Regement of Princes,* composed in 1411–1412, which place in the margin miniatures of Chaucer, and of these three, that in the Harley manuscript has been generally regarded as the most authentic. Except for the Ellesmere miniature, all the early likenesses of the poet seem to be more or less direct copies of the "Hoccleve

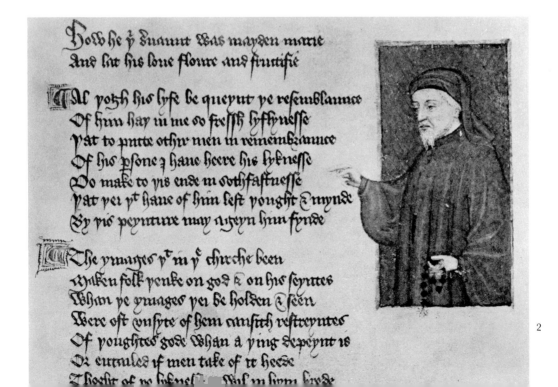

2

As in the Ellesmere portrait, a case for a writing implement hangs from the poet's neck; in his left hand he holds a string of prayer beads, betokening piety. See Spielmann, *Portraits of Chaucer,* pp. 6–10; *Text of the Canterbury Tales,* ed. Manly and Rickert, I, 587–90.

3. The Portrait with a Daisy

This miniature in MS British Museum Add. 5141, fol. 1, seems to be a late sixteenth-century descendant of a "Hoccleve portrait." Like other descendants, it has the beads in the left hand and the writing implement in the right, and the Chaucer arms in the upper left corner. In the upper right the date of death is mistakenly given as 1402, and below it is a daisy, presumably in reference to the poet's professed devotion to that flower. See Spielmann, *Portraits of Chaucer,* pp. 10f.

4. The Bodleian Portrait

In the Bodleian Library, Oxford, there is a descendant of the "Hoccleve" miniature, as is shown by the beads and the writing implement. But it is of crude workmanship and possesses little authority as a likeness. The hair and beard are darker in color, and the hood and robe are much lighter. Below the Chaucer coat-of-arms is inscribed in a very late hand "Caucer 1400." See Spielmann, *Portraits of Chaucer,* pp. 12f.

3

portrait." Hoccleve, a government clerk at Westminster, was a devoted disciple of Chaucer, who also had official duties about the palace, and he caused a miniaturist to portray the master in the margin opposite his tribute, which reads as follows:

Al thogh his lyfe be queynt the resemblaunce
Of him hath in me so fressh lyflynesse
That to putte othir men in remembraunce
Of his persone I have heere his lyknesse
Do make to this ende in sothfastnesse
That thei that have of him lest thought and mynde
By this peynture may ageyn him fynde.

4

5. The Harvard Portrait

This painting in oils on wood is in the Fogg Museum of Harvard University. It was, for three centuries at least, at Stanshawe's Court, near Bristol, and after passing through various hands was presented by Charles Eliot Norton to Harvard University as a memorial to two lovers of Chaucer, James Russell Lowell and Francis James Child. Probably executed late in the fifteenth century, it shows affinity to the Bodleian portrait and the portrait with a daisy in that all three show in the upper left corner the Chaucer arms, and all three show the string of beads and the writing implement in the poet's hands. It may be more authentic than the Bodleian painting since the beard is forked as in the earliest portraits, and the expression is somewhat more lifelike and slightly humorous. See Chaucer, *Canterbury Tales,* ed. J. M. Manly (New York, 1928), p. 38. Two portraits are not here reproduced, as lacking authority. That in the National Portrait Gallery is surely too crude a copy to be taken seriously, and that described by R. Call in *Speculum,* xxii (1947), 135–44, is too idealized. For the *Troilus* frontispiece showing Chaucer reciting to the court see Fig. 68.

5

6. Chaucer's Monument

The bones of Chaucer lie beneath the pavement of the south transept of Westminster Abbey, a privileged position not ordinarily granted to a civil servant or a poet. Was the favor due to Chaucer's close personal relationship to Bolingbroke, now Henry IV, and to his stepmother, Katherine, Chaucer's sister-in-law? Near the grave, set against the wall, is the original tomb with the poet's arms thrice repeated. Above it in 1556 an admirer, Nicholas Brigham, placed a marble canopy with four arches, enclosing a Latin inscription and a portrait. In 1652 Elias Ashmole published in *Theatrum Chemicum Britannicum* a copper engraving of the monument as it then was, though because the portrait was "somewhat decay'd," the engraver had restored it after an original "left to Posterity by his worthy Schollar Tho. Occleve." See E. P. Hammond, *Chaucer: A Bibliographical Manual* (New York, 1908, 1933), pp. 44–47; E. P. Kuhl, "Chaucer and Westminster Abbey," *Journal of English and Germanic Philology,* xlv (1946), 340–43; W. R. Lethaby, "Chaucer's Tomb," *Times Literary Supplement,* February 21, 1929, 137; *Royal Commission on Historical Monuments, An Inventory of Historical Monuments in London,* i (1924), p. 51, pl. 95. Owing to the precedent set by the burial of Chaucer in the south transept, other authors have been commemorated there, and it is known as "the Poets' Corner."

6

Cy comencent les croniques que fist maistre froissart qui parlent des nouuelles guerres de france et
dengleterre descoce et despaigne Lesquelles sont diuisees en quatre parties   Le prologue

Pour que honorables
auenues et nobles
auentures fais
darmes par les
guerres de france
et dengleterre
soient notablement
registrees et mis
en memoire per-
petuel parquoy
les preux ayent
exemple de culx encouragier en bien faisant
ie vueil traittier et proceder lystoire z matiere
de grant loenge dont ains que ie le comence
ie requier au sauueur de tout le monde qui
de neant crea toutes choses quil vueille creer
et mettre en moy sens et entendement si
vertueulx que ce liure que iay comence ie le
puisse continuer et perseuerer en tele maniere
que tous ceulx et celles qui le liront verront
et oront y puissent prendre esbatement
et plaisance et ie escheuir en leur grace Car
dist et vray est que tous edifices sont ouurez
et maconnez lune pierre apres lautre et

toutes grosses riuieres sont faictes et rassemblees de pluseurs sieux et pluseurs sourtdes
Aussi les sciences sont escriptes et complilees
de pluseurs clercz et ce que lun ne scet lautre
scet Non pourquant rien nest qui ne soit sceu
ou longz ou pres Dont aussi pour attaindre
et venir a la matiere que iay emprise de com-
mencier premierement de la grace de dieu
et de la benoite vierge marie dont tout cosort
et auancement vienment Je me vueil fonder
et ordonner sur les vrayes croniques iadis
faictes et rassemblees par venerable homme et
discret seigneur monss Iehan le bel chanoine
de saint lambert de liege qui grant cure et
toute bonne diligence mist en ceste matiere
et le continua tout son viuant au plus iuste-
ment quil pot et moult lui cousta a lacquerre
et a lauoir aiais quelz frais quil y eust ne
feist Riens ne les plaignoit car il estoit riche
et puissant si les pouoit bien porter et de soy
meismes large honnorable et courtois et
qui voulentiers vioit le sien despendre Aussi
il fu en son viuant moult ame et secrez a tres
noble et vaillie seigneur monss Iehan de

7

POETS WHOM CHAUCER ADMIRED

7. Froissart Presents a Book
to Richard II

Frontispiece of MS 804, Morgan Library, New York. Froissart's *Chronicle,* copied and illustrated by Guillaume de Bailly at Troyes about 1410. The miniature depicts two events related, respectively, near the beginning and the end of the book. On the right Queen Isabella of England, wearing a sideless *côte-hardie* and a skirt embroidered with the heraldic leopards of England and the lilies of France, holds the hand of her young son, the future Edward III, and presents him to her brother, Charles IV of France—an event of the year 1325. On the left Froissart kneels and gives Richard II a book of love poems—an event of the year 1395. The portraiture is unreliable. Among the poems may have been those which Chaucer echoed in the *Book of the Duchess* and the Prologue of the *Legend of Good Women,* namely, *Paradis Amoureus* (see Fig. 44), *Prison Amoureuse, Ditié de la Flour de la Margherite, Joli Mois de Mai.* Probably the two poets were acquainted, since Chaucer was in the service of King Edward in 1367 and Froissart had left the service of Queen Philippa only a short time earlier. Chaucer's name occurs in the *Chronicle* as a member of an important mission to France in 1377.

Clamantis, and *Confessio Amantis.* From 1378, when Chaucer, on leaving for Italy, gave him power of attorney, until 1385, when Chaucer paid him the great compliment of requesting his criticism of *Troilus,* the two poets must have been close friends. Gower repaid Chaucer by introducing a flattering reference to his youthful love songs in the first version of the *Confessio Amantis.* Perhaps the "moral Gower" was shocked by the coarser of the *Canterbury Tales;* at any rate he omitted the compliment in later editions of the *Confessio.*

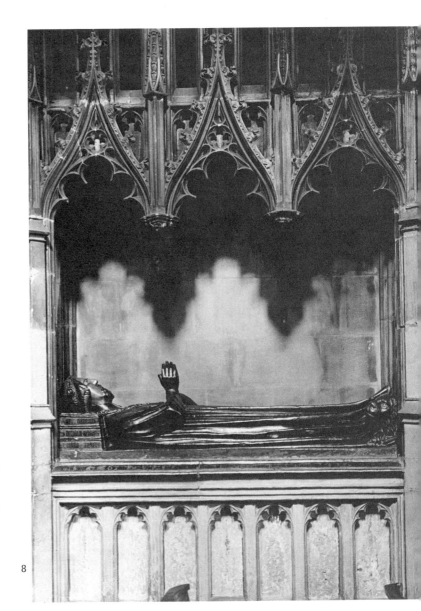

8. The Tomb of John Gower

O moral Gower, this book I directe
To the and to the, philosophical Strode,
To vouchen sauf, ther nede is, to correcte,
Of youre benignites and zeles goode.

Troilus, v, 1856–1859

Chaucer's friend, John Gower, was probably a well-to-do resident of Kent, passed the last years of his life in the precincts of the priory of St. Mary Overy in Surrey across London Bridge, and when he died in 1408 was buried in the priory church, now Southwark Cathedral. His monument represents the poet lying with his head resting on his three long poems, *Le Mirour de l'Homme, Vox*

9

9. Guillaume de Machaut

Miniature in MS Bibl. Nat. fr. 1584. The volume, dated ca. 1370, contains the works of Machaut. The miniature, illustrating a scene in the Prologue, shows the poet seated beside a lectern furnished with books. The winged God of Love approaches, leading his son *Doux Penser* (Sweet Thought) and his daughters, *Plaisance* (Joy) and *Esperance* (Hope). Machaut enjoyed a great reputation not only as a technician in verse but also as a musical composer. His *Jugement du Roi de Behaigne* (Bohemia), *Jugement du Roi de Navarre,* and *Dit de la Fontaine Amoureuse* influenced the *Book of the Duchess,* and his *Dit de la Marguerite* influenced the Prologue of the *Legend of Good Women.*

10. Deschamps Kneeling before King Charles VI

A miniature in MS Bibl. Nat. fr. 20029, fol. 4v. A presentation copy of Deschamps's poems, dated 1383. Deschamps is represented offering the book to the demented king, Charles VI. His career paralleled that of Chaucer in several ways. He studied law, became attached to the court, traveled widely, and was sent on missions. Possibly Chaucer, during his imprisonment by the French, met Deschamps at Rheims in 1359 or 1360, but it is certain that he knew and borrowed from the latter's *Miroir de Mariage.* In 1386, apparently in response to an overture of some kind, the French poet sent to the English poet by the hand of Sir Lewis Clifford a highly complimentary *balade.* See Chaucer, *Canterbury Tales,* ed. J. M. Manly (New York, 1928), pp. 22–25, and Brusendorff, *Chaucer Tradition,* pp. 485–93.

I COELVM CECINIT MEDIVMQVE IMVMQVE TRIBVNALS   LVSTRAVIT QVE ANIMO CVNCTA POETA SVO   DOCTVS ADEST DANTES SVA QVEM FLORENTIA SAEPE
ISIT CONSILIIS AC PIETATE PATREM   NIL POTVIT TANTO MORS SAEVA NOCERE POETAE   QVEM VIVVM VIRTVS CARMEN IMAGO FACIT

11. Dante, the *Commedia,* and the City of Florence

Wel kan the wise poete of Florence,
That highte Dant, speken in this sentence.
                    Wife of Bath's Tale, 1125f.

A painting in the Duomo, Florence, executed by Domenico di Michelino in 1465. See R. T. Holbrook, *Portraits of Dante from Giotto to Raffael* (London, Boston, New York, 1911), pp. 172–81. On the right, within the walls, are clearly recognizable the Duomo, the machicolated tower of the Palazzo Vecchio, and Giotto's bell tower, all of which Chaucer must have seen when he visited Florence in 1373, and which we can see today. In the middle is a fairly authentic portrait of Dante, crowned with laurel, holding the *Commedia* and pointing to the gate of hell and the damned being herded by devils. On his right rises the mountain of Purgatory, where repentant sinners are purged by suffering. At the top is the Garden of Eden, anachronistically identified by the figures of Adam and Eve. The celestial Paradise is represented by bands arching over all, distinguished by five luminaries, the sun and the planets of the Ptolemaic cosmos. A painting of the Inferno, showing Dante, Virgil, and Count Ugolino, is reproduced in Fig. 176.

12

12. Petrarch

I wol yow telle a tale which that I
Lerned at Padowe of a worthy clerk,
As preved by his wordes and his werk. . . .

Fraunceys Petrak, the lauriat poete,
Highte this clerk, whos rethorike sweete
Enlumyned al Ytaille of poetrie.

Clerk's Prologue, 26–33

Portrait from MS Bibl. Nat. lat. 6069F, fol. Av. *De Viris Illustribus,* date 1379, five years after the poet's death. It is possible, though unlikely, that Chaucer during his visit to Italy in the spring of 1373 met Petrarch, who as early as 1341 had been crowned with laurel at Rome and had since achieved a reputation throughout Europe as scholar and man of letters. It is certain that, besides referring to Petrarch as above, Chaucer translated the song of Troilus (Book I, 400–20) from his sonnet 88, and used his Latin version of the story of Griselda, together with an anonymous French version, as the basis of the Clerk's Tale. See Severs in *Sources and Analogues of the "Canterbury Tales,"* ed. Bryan and Dempster (Chicago, 1941), pp. 288–331.

PEOPLE WHOM CHAUCER KNEW

13

13. Edward III and His Sons Kneeling before the Virgin

A copy made by Richard Smirke, in the possession of the Society of Antiquaries, of a wall painting (since destroyed by fire) in St. Stephen's Chapel, Westminster Palace. Date 1350–1363. The damaged upper part showed the Virgin enthroned, one magus kneeling and another standing before her, while a third approaches. At the left attendants with swords, and a groom holding the reins of a horse are to be seen. Below, St. George, the patron saint of England, presents Edward III to the Virgin. Kneeling behind the king are his sons, the Black Prince, Lionel, John of Gaunt, Edmund, and Thomas. Reproduced by permission of the Society of Antiquaries. See John T. Smith, *Antiquities of Westminster* (London, 1807), pp. 158f; Henry Shaw, *Dresses and Decorations of the Middle Ages* (London, 1843), I, unnumbered plate; E. W. Tristram, *English Wall Painting of the Fourteenth Century* (London, 1955), pp. 48–58.

14. The Tomb of Edward III

The gilded bronze effigy of Edward III was cast in the year of his death, 1377, and lies on his tomb in Westminster Abbey. Two scepters which he held have been broken off, but the figure remains a superb piece of stylized portraiture. See *Royal Commission on Historical Monuments, London,* I (1924), 30; pl. 187. The poet's father, John Chaucer, in the year 1338 was commanded by King Edward to accompany the royal household to Flanders and the Rhineland, probably in the capacity of an expert in wines at a time when water was a dangerous beverage; later we find him deputy to the King's Butler at Southampton. Probably this vinous connection with the royal household explains Geoffrey's appearance as a page in the household of Prince Lionel in 1357 and the king's payment of sixteen pounds for his ransom from the French in 1360. In 1367 a document signed by Edward granted him a pension and referred to him as "dilectus valettus noster." From that time until 1377 Chaucer seems to have been

employed on confidential missions, bringing him into close relationship with the aging king. At the Garter Feast of 1374 he received the extraordinary grant of a pitcher of wine to be taken daily from the king's butler, a sign of special favor.

15. The Effigy of Queen Philippa

As a matter of policy Edward III married Philippa of Hainault in 1327, and she bore him many sons and daughters. In 1366 her image was carved in white marble by Hennequin of Liège; it was placed on her tomb in Westminster Abbey three years before her death of the plague in 1369. Unfortunately the tomb and the hands of the queen have been badly damaged, and a curious projecting headdress obscures her face. See *Royal Commission on Historical Monuments, London,* I (1924), 30; pl. 187. Chaucer makes no mention of Queen Philippa, but it is possible that her intervention in behalf of the burghers of Calais in 1347 may have been preserved in tradition and may have inspired the pleading of Ypolita with Theseus for Arcite and Palamon in the Knight's Tale. See G. G. Coulton, *Chaucer and His England,* Ch. XIV.

16. Lionel Duke of Clarence

A gilt bronze portrait figure of Lionel Duke of Clarence, with coat of arms below, from the tomb of his father, Edward III, in Westminster Abbey. Date 1377. See *Royal Commission on Historical Monuments, London,* I (1924), 30. Twenty years earlier than the casting of this figure, as the records show, Chaucer was in the service, probably as a page, of Lionel's wife, Elizabeth Countess of Ulster; he was probably in their train as they traveled from London and Windsor in 1357 to Woodstock, Doncaster, and their seat at Hatfield, Yorkshire, where

they stayed from July to the end of March 1358. In April of that year he may have been in attendance for a second time at the great feast of the Order of the Garter at Windsor, when Lionel and the Countess were present, and King Edward entertained the King of Cyprus and the captive kings of France and Scotland. Later in the year we find Lionel's household in Anglesey, at Liverpool, Reading, London, and, during Lent of 1359, at Hatfield once more. In the French campaign that followed, Chaucer, probably in Lionel's contingent, was captured near Rheims. On the campaign see Emerson in *Romanic Review,* III (1912),

328, 337–41, 352–61. After his release he was employed by Lionel to carry letters from Calais to England. Thus it was in this princely entourage that the poet traveled in England, Wales, and France, and received his first lessons in courtly behavior, warfare, and diplomacy.

17. John of Gaunt

Miniature in MS British Museum Nero D vii, fol. 7. A donation book, listing the benefactors of St. Albans Abbey, north of London, together with their portraits. Date of the miniature ca. 1380. The Duke, who was then about forty years old, is depicted kneeling in a *tabernacle* (architectural niche), with a chaplet round his head and a piece of cloth of gold draped over a monument. The inscription reads: "Johannes dux Lancastrie pro anima domine Blanchie uxoris sue, cuius corpus hic pernoctavit, contulit huic ecclesie duos pannos aureos." ("John, Duke of Lancaster, gave to this church for the soul of Blanche, his wife, whose body lay here one night [on its way to London], two pieces of cloth of gold.") This gift, as well as the tender mention of the Duchess in John's instructions for his own burial by her side, bear

17

witness to the fact that the marriage, though dictated originally by politics, was also a love match. See Fig. 18. On the manuscript see Galbraith in *English Historical Review*, XLVII (1932), 13f.

It was late in 1357 that John of Gaunt, seventeen years old, probably first set eyes on a somewhat younger stripling, a page in the household of his brother and sister-in-law, Lionel and Elizabeth, at their mansion at Hatfield, Yorkshire. See Fig. 16. Twelve years later, when the Duke returned from his campaign in France, his beloved wife had died of the plague, and it was the former page who composed a tender elegy, the *Book of the Duchess*. In 1372, when the Duke married Constance, the daughter of Petro of Castile (see Fig. 141), Chaucer's wife, Philippa, became one of her ladies-in-waiting in the splendid palace of the Savoy. The degree of favor which Geoffrey and Philippa enjoyed is indicated by a joint pension of ten pounds which they received from the Duke in 1374, and by the fact that in 1389 their son, Thomas Chaucer, was received into his service. The death of John of Gaunt, "time-honored Lancaster," in 1399 brought to an end a friendly relationship with the poet that seems to have begun forty-two years before. See J. R. Hulbert, *Chaucer's Official Life* (Menasha, 1912), pp. 58–63.

18. The Tomb of John of Gaunt and Blanche the Duchess

An engraving from W. Dugdale, *History of St. Paul's Cathedral in London*, 2nd ed. (London, 1716), p. 90. In 1374, five years after the Duchess' death and twenty-five years before his own, John of Gaunt

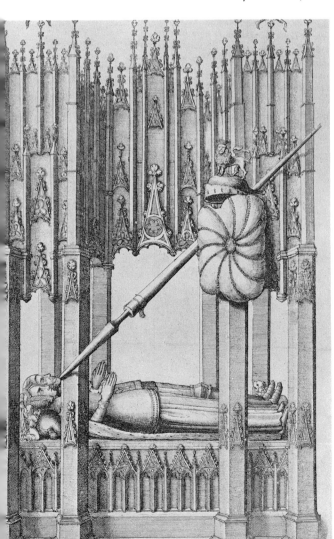

arranged for the making of alabaster effigies and the erection of a tomb in St. Paul's Cathedral by Yevele, the master mason, and Thomas Wreck. In his will he directed, first of all, that his body be buried beside his "very dear erstwhile comrade [*compaigne*] Blanche." On Blanche, see M. Anderson in *Modern Philology,* XLV (1948), 152–59. On

the tomb see G. H. Cook, *Old St. Paul's Cathedral* (London, 1955), pp. 53f, 57. As we see in the engraving, a spear, a decorative shield, and the cap and crest which adorned a helm (possibly those which the Duke had actually carried or worn) were suspended from the stone canopy of the tomb.

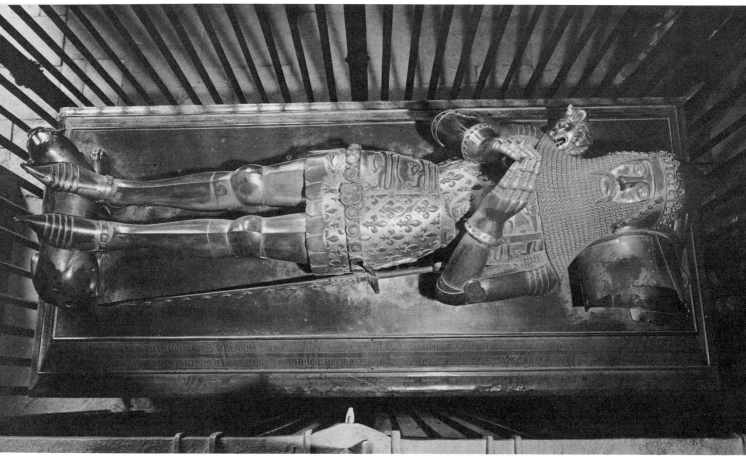

19

19. The Effigy of the Black Prince

Edward, the Black Prince, eldest son of Edward III, was the hero of the great victories at Crecy (1346) and Poitiers (1356) over the French. Before his departure in 1363 to take over his Duchy of Aquitaine and after his return in 1371 he must have been fairly well known to Chaucer, and his widow, Joan of Kent (Fig. 20) had several close friends in common with the poet. The Prince died in 1376, his body lay in state in Westminster Hall, and now his effigy in gilded bronze lies on his tomb in Canterbury Cathedral in an attitude of

prayer. His *gypon* (tunic) is embroidered with the heraldic leopards of England and the fleur-de-lis of France, while his head rests on a helm and his feet on a hound. Until 1939 a shield, a crested helm, a scabbard, and gauntlets, which the Prince may actually have used in his lifetime (the helm bears the marks of blows), were suspended over his tomb, but are now replaced by replicas. See C. A. Stothard, *Monumental Effigies of Great Britain,* new edition by J. Hewitt (London, 1876), pp. 118–24; *Edward the Black Prince,* Canterbury Papers No. 8 (revised 1963).

20. Princess Joan of Kent

Miniature from MS. British Museum Nero D vii, fol. 7v. Donation Book of St. Albans Abbey. Date of this miniature ca. 1380. Joan, known as "the Fair Maid of Kent," was a celebrated beauty. By her second marriage she became Countess of Salisbury, and it was probably in her honor that an enamored Edward III founded the Order of the Garter in 1348. A widow, she married in 1361 Edward's eldest son, the Black Prince. On his death in 1376 she exercised a considerable and beneficent influence during the minority of her son Richard II and thereafter until her death in 1385. Chaucer's close friend, Lewis Clifford, was in her entourage, and the poet himself received mourning costume to wear at her funeral. How faithful a likeness the miniature is, we can never know. The Princess is shown pointing to a gold

brooch which she gave to the Abbey. The inscription reads: "Domina Johanna principissa magnis oblationibus sepius martirem honoravit, inter quas nobile monile aureum ei dedit et pro caritate conventui centum solidos assignavit." ("The lady Princess Joan very often honored the martyr [St. Alban] with great offerings, among which she gave him a noble golden brooch and for charity granted to the monastery a hundred shillings.") On this miniature see *English Historical Review,* XLVII (1932), 12ff.; V. H. Galbraith, *St. Albans Chronicle* (Oxford, 1937), pp. xxxvi f.; J. Harvey, *The Plantagenets* (1948), pl. 44.

21. The Effigies of Richard II and Anne of Bohemia

These effigies, which lie on a tomb in Westminster Abbey, were ordered by King Richard on April 24, 1395, and were cast in bronze and gilded by two coppersmiths of London. See T. Rymer, *Foedera* (London, 1709), VII, 797f.; *Royal Commission on Historical Monuments, London,* I (1924), 31. Queen Anne had died the previous year, and Richard died in 1400. Chaucer seems to have been in favor with the king from his accession in 1377 to his departure for Ireland in 1399, and in *Lack of Steadfastness* ventured to counsel him. In *Troilus* there seems to be a reference to Anne in Book I, line 171 ("Right as oure firste lettre is now an A"), and in all probability the *Legend of Good Women* was written at her request. The beautiful frontispiece to *Troilus* (Fig. 68) depicts Chaucer reciting before the royal couple and their court.

INVENTION OF PAINTING IN OYLE 1410 THIS WAS PAINTED BEFORE
THE BEGINING OF RIC. 2d. 1377

22. Richard II Adoring the Virgin and Child

This painting, called the Wilton Diptych, is in the National Gallery, London, and is generally rated as the supreme example of English Gothic painting. At the left stand three patron saints, King Edmund of East Anglia, King Edward the Confessor, and John the Baptist, with their respective emblems of arrow, ring, and lamb. King Richard, kneeling, is robed in red, brocaded in gold with his badge of a hart in a circle of broompods; he wears a collar with the same device. In the right panel the Virgin stands in a flowery meadow, surrounded by eleven garlanded angels, each wearing a necklace of broompods and Richard's badge of the white hart. One holds the banner of St. George, patron saint of England. The infant Christ extends

22

his arms in a welcoming gesture. The faces of St. Edward and St. Edmund were probably painted to resemble Edward III and the Black Prince, Richard's grandfather and father. Richard's face is that of a youth in his late teens or early twenties, and this raises a difficulty, for the device of broompods was not adopted till 1395 or 1396. Expert opinion is divided between (1) assigning the painting to this date and (2) regarding it as an ideal portrait of Richard in his youth, but painted after his death and referring to his welcome by the Queen of Heaven. See Thomas Bodkin, *The Wilton Diptych* (London, 1947); F. Wormald in *Journal of the Warburg and Courtauld Institutes,* XVII (1954), 191–202; John H. Harvey in *Archaeologia,* XCVIII (1961), 1–28.

23

Chaucer from a charge of "raptus." See on Philipot's career *Dictionary of National Biography*, xv, 1045–47. See on his association with Chaucer, Kuhl in *Philological Quarterly*, xxv (1946), 277–80. There could be no stronger guarantor of Chaucer's probity of character than Philipot.

24. Bernabo Visconti

> Off Melan grete Barnabo Viscounte,
> God of delit, and scourge of Lumbardye,
> Why sholde I nat thyn infortune acounte?
>
> Monk's Tale, 2399–2401

Equestrian statue of Bernabo, tyrant of Milan, made in 1363 by Bonino da Campione, now in the Castello Sforzesco, Milan. The *gypon* (tunic) is adorned with the arms of the Visconti family, appropriately an adder. These powerful and

23. Sir John Philipot, Merchant

Miniature in MS British Museum Nero D vii, fol. 105v. Date ca. 1380. The donation book of St. Albans Abbey. The inscription reads: "Johannes Philipott, civis Londoniarum, contulit ad idem opus [claustri] xx libros. Dedit et duas summas dactilorum et amigdalorum." ("John Philipot, citizen of London, gave to the same work [of the cloister] 20 pounds. He also gave two loads of dates and almonds.") Philipot's occupation is indicated by a money bag, and he was not only one of the wealthiest merchants of England, but also in the early years of Richard's reign an outstanding national figure. Mayor of London in 1378, he fitted out at his own expense a fleet which cleared the channel of French raiders. See General Prologue, 276, describing the Merchant: "He wolde the see were kept for any thyng. . . ." In 1381 Philipot was knighted by King Richard for his services during the Peasants' Revolt. Chaucer, also descended from the merchant class, must have had close official and friendly relations with him. For six years (1378–1384) the poet, as Controller of the Customs on Wools and Hides for the port of London, was the superior of Philipot, who was one of the Collectors of these customs. On the other hand, it was from Philipot, acting as one of the treasurers for war with France, that Chaucer received £66. 13. 4 for his expenses on the diplomatic journey to Milan in 1378. And in 1380 Philipot, together with Sir John Clanvowe and Sir William Neville, witnessed a deed exonerating

wealthy lords of Milan had for generations been notorious for their poisonings and assassinations, and in 1385 Bernabo was murdered by his nephew. In 1368 his niece was married with great pomp to Chaucer's patron, Prince Lionel, who very shortly died. Ten years later Chaucer was sent as a member of a very important diplomatic mission to Milan to deal with this sinister character and with Sir John Hawkwood, the English captain of mercenaries operating in Italy. On the statue see *Storia di Milano* (1955), Giovanni Treccani degli Alfieri, v, pp. 2, 421, 530, 808f. On Chaucer's mission see Kuhl in *Modern Language Notes,* LXII (1947), 42–44.

25

25. Bolingbroke Delivering Richard II to the Londoners

O conquerour of Brutes Albyon . . . !
Complaint of Chaucer to His Purse, 22

Miniature in MS British Museum Harley 1319. *Chronicle* of Jean Creton, French workmanship, ca. 1400. Richard II, on his return from Ireland in August 1399, was treacherously captured by Bolingbroke, John of Gaunt's son, whom he had disinherited, and was brought to London. There he was delivered to the mayor and citizens, as we see in the miniature. Bolingbroke is fully armed, except for the tall black hat on his head. Richard strongly resembles in feature and costume the effigy on his tomb in Westminster Abbey (Fig. 21). Later he was forced to abdicate in Westminster Hall, and Bolingbroke was crowned as Henry IV. On the manuscript and the miniatures see *Burlington Magazine,* v (1904), 160–72, 267–78; *Archaeologia,* xx (1824), 1–242. Bolingbroke, as John of Gaunt's son, must long have been on familiar terms with Chaucer. In 1396 he gave the poet a splendid scarlet robe, trimmed with fur, and on the very day of his coronation in 1399 he confirmed the annuity granted by his predecessor.

PLACES AND BUILDINGS WHICH CHAUCER KNEW

26. London in 1547

A water-color copy in the possession of the Society of Antiquaries at Burlington House, London, of a painting made by Hieronym Grimm, showing the royal procession from the Tower to Westminster the day before the coronation of Edward VI. See W. H. St. John Hope, *Cowdray and Eastbourne Priory* (London, 1919), pp. 56f. Though the costumes had changed greatly since Chaucer's day, the general aspect of the city was much the same, and the main landmarks are still recognizable. Beginning at the left, we see the Tower, surrounded by the Thames and a moat; the bridge across the Thames; the conspicuous bell tower of St. Mary-le-Bow; across the river, St. Mary Overy (now Southwark Cathedral); the main street, Cheapside (*Chepe*) with its cross; St. Paul's Cathedral; Ludgate; then (much foreshortened) Temple Bar, Charing Cross, and Westminster Palace.

27. Westminster and Charing Cross, ca. 1550

A drawing by Antonie van den Wyngaerde in the British Museum, Map 184. f2, showing the western fringe of London, and the Palace and Abbey of Westminster much as Chaucer had known them more than 150 years earlier. On the right, on the bank of the Thames, is the Hospital of the Blessed Mary of Rouncivalle, for the benefit of which, ostensibly, the Pardoner was collecting funds. To the left of this rises Charing Cross, a stone monument erected in 1291 by Edward I near the spot where Queen Eleanor's coffin rested on its way to Westminster Abbey for interment. At the left of

the picture, on the site of the present Houses of Parliament, are the buildings of the King's Palace, with which the poet must have been very familiar from 1367 to the end of his life. The two-storied pinnacled structure on the river bank is the chapel of St. Stephen, adorned with paintings of Edward III and his sons (Fig. 13). To the right of it is the long low roof of Westminster Hall (Fig. 30) and the high roof of the abbey church, where the royal tombs and Chaucer's monument are placed. Under the inscription "Palace Gate" is the towered entrance to the precincts. Jutting out into the river is a landing stage used for boat traffic to the city of London.

27

28. The Tower of London and the Bridge

A miniature in the Flemish style, dated ca. 1500, in MS British Museum, Royal 16 F ii, fol. 73, a collection of the poems of Charles Duc d'Orléans. Captured by the English at the battle of Agincourt (1415), the duke spent twenty-five years as a prisoner in England. In the miniature he appears three times, writing at a table, looking out of a window, and dispatching a messenger. See Warner and Gilson, *Catalogue of the Royal and King's Manuscripts in the British Museum,* II (1921), 203f. Filling most of the space in the miniature is the group of buildings—including the whitewashed keep of William the Conqueror's time and the water gate on the Thames—called the Tower. Between 1389 and 1391 Chaucer, as Clerk of the King's Works, was responsible for its maintenance and repairs. Seen above the keep are the arcaded warehouses of Billingsgate on the river front. To the left of these is London Bridge, uniting the city with Southwark; it is flanked with houses and supports a chapel, rebuilt in 1384 and dedicated to the martyred St. Thomas. Chaucer must have crossed the bridge many times.

29. The Interior of the Temple Church

This church, damaged by incendiary bombs in World War II, was originally built by the Knights Templars outside the walls of London as a round structure in imitation of the so-called Temple of Solomon at Jerusalem. It was consecrated in 1185. Chaucer was presumably familiar with this building in his early twenties. When the Order of the Templars was dissolved in 1312, their church was assigned to the Hospitallers, but the adjacent property was taken over by a society of lawyers and used in part as a law school. Here, in all probability, Chaucer was a student between 1360 and 1367, since a record of the Inner Temple, now lost but well authenticated, certifies that he was fined for beating a friar in Fleet Street. On the church see *Royal Commission on Historical Monuments, London,* IV (1929), 137–41; on Chaucer's connection with the Inner Temple see E. Rickert in *J. M. Manly Anniversary Studies* (Chicago, 1923), pp. 20–31.

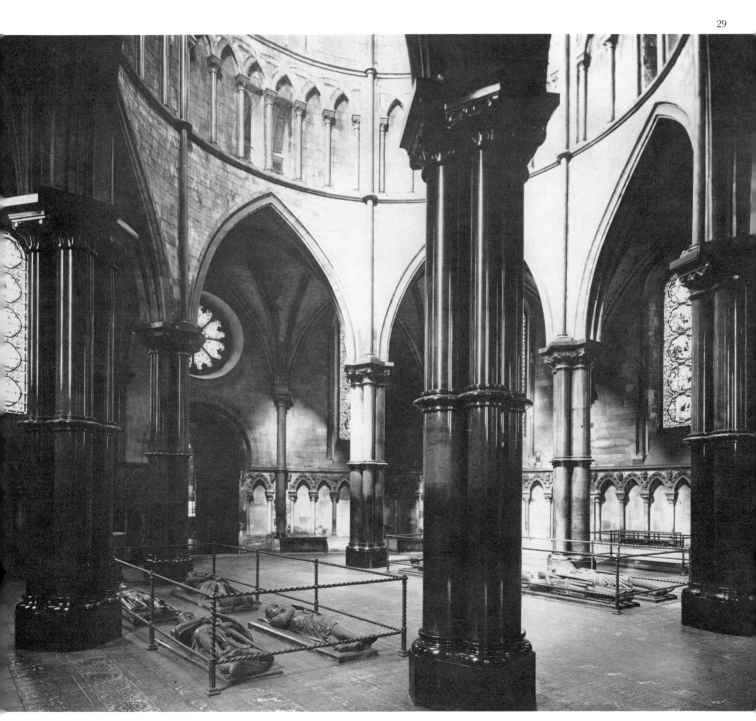

30

30. The Hall of Westminster Palace

The walls of this historic edifice still incorporate some of the original stonework used in the original hall of King William Rufus (1087–1100). Chaucer, while in the service of King Edward III (1367–1374), must have been very familiar with every part of the royal palace, and again as Clerk of the King's Works (1389–1391). In 1393 his successor in the post ordered oak timbers for the roof, which was designed by the master craftsman Henry Yevele and constructed in 1395–1396. Except for necessary replacements this is the roof we see today, a masterpiece of Gothic woodwork, which Chaucer must have seen and admired in his last years. See J. H. Harvey, *Henry Yevele* (London, 1944), pp. 47–51; *Royal Commission on Historical Monuments, Westminster* (1925), pp. 121–23; *Journal of the British Archaeological Association*, ser. 3, I (1937), 168–228. Westminster Hall has been the scene of many dramatic events in the history of England, none more so than the forced abdication of Richard II in 1399 under the newly constructed roof here shown, about a year before Chaucer's death. On the Court of Common Pleas, which held its sessions in Westminster Hall, see Fig. 31.

31. The Court of Common Pleas at Westminster

One of four miniatures in the Library of the Inner Temple, extracted from a book of law terms and depicting the superior courts at Westminster. Date ca. 1460. The Court of Common Pleas held its sessions in a part of the great hall of the royal palace of Westminster (see Fig. 30), and Chaucer must have attended them more than once. See on the miniatures *Archaeologia,* xxxix, part 2 (1863), 360f., 369, and Margaret Hastings, *The Court of Common Pleas in Fifteenth Century England* (Ithaca, N.Y., 1947), colored frontispiece and pp. 28–30. Thomas Pynchbek, who as justice in assize may

have served as a model for Chaucer's Sergeant of the Law, later became justice in the Court of Common Pleas, which dealt with civil cases involving property, debt, etc. See J. M. Manly, *Some New Light on Chaucer* (New York, 1926), pp. 131–57. The miniature, reproduced by permission of the Masters of the Bench of the Inner Temple, shows at the top three shields with, respectively, (1) the arms ascribed to Edward the Confessor (pre-Conquest England); (2) the leopards of England combined with the lilies of France (England after Edward III claimed the crown of

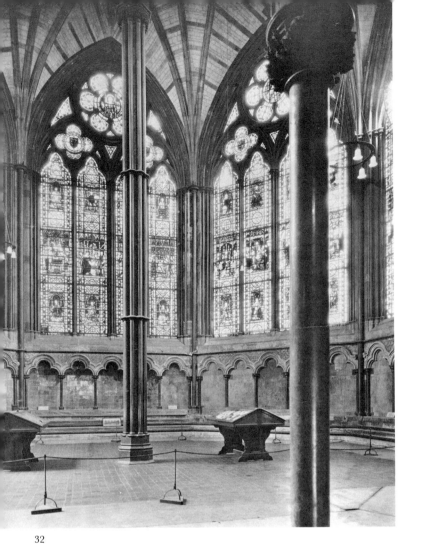

32

32. The Chapter House, Westminster

In this meeting place of the monks of Westminster Abbey it was customary, from the end of Edward III's reign to the last years of Richard II's, for the House of Commons to hold its sittings. Here Chaucer's Franklin would have had a place on the stone bench which ran around the wall, and here the poet himself would have spent some very anxious days as Knight of the Shire from Kent in the autumn of 1386 when Richard was engaged in a bitter struggle for power with parliament, led by his uncle Thomas, Duke of Gloucester. See *Journal of the British Archaeological Association,* ser. 3, III (1938), 117. It was not many yards from here, in the south transept of the church, that Chaucer was buried fourteen years later. In spite of restorations the chapter house, with its marble columns and tile paving, retains much of the beauty which it possessed when it was built about 1250. See *Royal Commission on Historical Monuments, London,* I, 79.

33. Windsor Castle

A drawing by Hollar, a Bohemian etcher (1607–1677), shows Windsor Castle much as it was in Chaucer's time, before the extensive alterations made in the eighteenth and nineteenth centuries. Presumably, as a page in the household of Elizabeth, wife of Lionel Duke of Clarence, Chaucer participated in the splendid festivities held by Edward III in the castle on St. George's Day (April 23) in 1357 and 1358. In 1390, when he was in his middle forties, he was commissioned to oversee urgent repairs to St. George's Chapel. (The present St. George's Chapel was built about a hundred years later.) See W. H. St. John Hope, *Windsor Castle* (London, 1913), I, 221; II, 374f.

France); (3) the leopards alone (Plantagenet England). Below the shields sit seven judges wearing red robes and white coifs. At the table covered with green cloth nine clerks keep record on scrolls of parchment, and at each end is a crier with a staff. At the bottom is a long-haired defendant in a smock, attended by an officer bearing a staff. Five sergeants at law in blue and green robes and white coifs stand on either side of this pair.

33

THE ARTS OF METALWORK

In spite of several visitations of the bubonic plague, the interruptions of war, and the consequent poverty, the arts of metalwork seem to have flourished in Chaucer's lifetime with scarcely diminished vigor and splendor. There are the royal effigies at Westminster and Canterbury, illustrated above. In sacristies and museums we see crucifixes, croziers, and sacramental vessels of the period, though considerably diminished in numbers by the Reformation. Reduced even more drastically by time are the once multitudinous pieces of secular plate, gleaming with gilding, enamels, and precious stones, which adorned the festal board (see Figs. 163, 165). On the other hand, thousands of bronze memorial plates of the fourteenth and fifteenth centuries, known as brasses, still adorn the floors and tombs of English churches. Even the humbler craftsmen and the minters of coin often displayed a masterly sense of design.

34. The King's Lynn Goblet

In the Guildhall at King's Lynn is a wonderfully preserved silver-gilt cup for the service of the table. Like the royal gold goblet in the British Museum (Fig. 35), it is adorned with translucent enamels, but the subjects represented are courtly figures in the costume of the middle of the fourteenth century, a few years after Chaucer was born. It was probably made by English craftsmen. See N. M. Penzer in *Connoisseur,* cxviii (1946), 10–12, 64, 79–84.

35. A Royal Goblet

A goblet of solid gold in the British Museum is fitted with a lid; both lid and goblet are decorated with translucent enameling. The decorations illustrate scenes from the life and miracles of St. Agnes, a virgin martyr like St. Cecilia. On the cover she is represented kneeling among the flames. On the bowl she appears with three other virgin martyrs, all haloed, to her family. On the stem is a winged figure, symbolizing the evangelist Matthew. In its original state, here reconstructed in an outline drawing, the goblet was adorned with sapphires, rubies, and many pearls, and of these last some still remain. Mentioned in various documents, this royal goblet has a fairly complete history. Proba-

35

bly executed for Jean Duc de Berry about 1380, it was donated to his nephew, Charles VI, in 1391. After the occupation of Paris by the English it came into the possession of John Duke of Bedford, the Regent, subsequently passed to his heir, King Henry VI, and remained in the royal treasury until 1604.

36. A Bell-Metal Jug

This jug in the Victoria and Albert Museum (No. 217, 1879) was cast about 1380, apparently for service in the royal household, since it bears the royal arms of leopards and lilies surmounted by a crown. The hospitable inscription reads: "GODDIS GRACE BE IN THIS PLACE AMEN +

STOND UTTIR [away] FROM THE FYRE AND LAT ON LUST [let anyone who pleases] COME NERE."

36

37. William of Wykeham's Crozier

William of Wykeham (1324-1404), Bishop of Winchester and twice Chancellor of England, was one of the outstanding personages in the kingdom between 1367 and 1376 and between 1389 and 1391. He first commended himself to King Edward III by his oversight of the buildings at Windsor Castle (see Fig. 33) in the 1350's. In the 1380's he founded New College, Oxford, for the training of priests, and is generally credited with the architectural plan (see Fig. 55). He bequeathed to the college his crozier, now preserved in the chapel. The head and the spike at the foot of this splendid example of silver and enamel work are reproduced here. Also of exquisite workmanship is a brooch, twice depicted, formed in the shape of the letter *M*, standing for Maria, enclosing small figures of the Virgin and the angel of the Annunciation. See on the subject of the crozier and jewel *Archaeologia*, LX (1907), part 2, pp. 465–72.

37

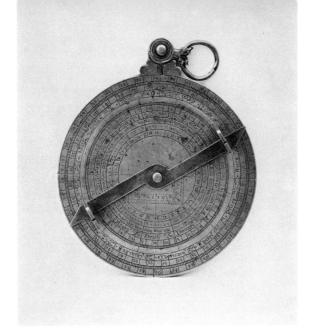

38

38, 39. An Astrolabe

Chaucer's interest in astronomy is attested by his *Treatise on the Astrolabe* (1391). In *The Astrolabes of the World* (Oxford, 1932), ii, 482, R. P. T. Gunther says that an astrolabe, reproduced here, formerly at Painswick, Gloucestershire, and now in the Museum of Science, Oxford, "is an excellent example of the type figured in the Chaucerian manuscripts." See P. Pintelon, *Chaucer's Treatise on the Astrolabe* (Antwerp, 1940).

40. Coins

Of the coins mentioned by Chaucer, six are depicted here in the original size, by courtesy of the American Numismatic Society. The gold noble (*a*) of Edward III's reign, also current in Richard II's, had the value of 6s. 8d., or a third of a pound. Minted in the Tower of London, it shows Edward standing in a ship, sword in hand, crown on head, a shield with the leopards of England and the lilies of France on his left side. These arms were adopted in 1340, and the great naval victory over the French fleet in the same year probably suggested the ship. About fifty years later Chaucer referred to the coin in the Miller's Tale, 3255f., describing Alison: "Ful brighter was the shynyng of hir hewe Than in the Tour the noble yforged newe."

39

The shield (*b*), or *écu d'or*, was a French gold coin, worth half a noble. It depicted a king enthroned, scepter in hand, and a shield with the lilies of France at his left. Hence the name. Though in England it was illegal to deal in them, the Merchant of Chaucer's Prologue (278) did so: "Wel koude he in eschaunge sheeldes selle."

The florin (*d*), minted originally in Florence, presented on one face a lily and on the other John the Baptist—the floral arms and the patron saint of that city. Florins were in wide circulation on the European continent, including Flanders, and should be distinguished from English coins of the same name. The three Flemish rioters in the Pardoner's Tale (770) found a horde "of floryns fyne of gold ycoyned rounde."

The groat, the penny, and the farthing (*c, e, f*), all silver coins, are mentioned with contempt by the friar in the Summoner's Tale (1964–67). "A! yif that covent foure and twenty grotes! A! yif that frere a peny and lat hym go! Nay, nay, Thomas, it may no thyng be so! What is a ferthyng worth parted in twelve!" Four farthings made a penny, and four pence made a groat.

One must not be misled by the present-day purchasing power of the English penny. In the late fourteenth century it must have had the value of at least ten shillings, equivalent to $1.50 in 1965; the gold noble would have been worth at least forty pounds, or $120 at today's rate of exchange.

40

a   b   c   d   e   f

41. A Feast Scene Incised on a "Brass"

A detail of the monumental "brass" of Robert Braunche, twice mayor of King's Lynn, and his successive wives. Set in the pavement of St. Margaret's church in that town, the great sheet of bronze representing the three figures was probably designed and cut in North Germany to order, shortly before or shortly after Braunche's death in 1364. Twenty years earlier King Edward III visited King's Lynn with his court, and if Braunche entertained them, the event is probably commemorated in the feast scene depicted in the space below his feet. Here we see a king seated at the left, while dignitaries and their wives fill the rest of the table. On the right, however, a man is straddling the table in most undignified fashion to take a platter of roast peacock from a serving lady. At the extreme left three ladies approach the table, one bearing a peacock. According to custom, musicians lend cheer to the banquet. For a description see H. W. Macklin, *Brasses of England* (London, 1907), pp. 84–89.

THE ROMAUNT OF THE ROSE

42. The Garden of the Rose

> I saugh a gardyn right anoon,
> Ful long and brood, and everydell
> Enclosed was, and walled well
> With highe walles enbatailled,
> Portraied without and wel entailled
> With many riche portraitures.
>
> *Romaunt of the Rose,* 136–41

A page in MS British Museum Egerton 1069, fol. 1. Below, the artist has depicted the dreaming poet in bed. Above, we see the river; the dreamer admitted by Idleness to the garden; the battlemented wall, on which are portrayed *Couvoitise* (Covetousness), with a mantle draped over a rack, *Avarice,* with a treasure chest, *Envie,* and *Tristece* (Sorrow). Within the wall, to the left is *Daunger* (Haughtiness), a churlish figure with a club. In the middle is the spring that feeds the river, and Narcissus, gazing at his reflection. On the manuscript see H. L. D. Ward, *Catalogue of Romances in the Department of Manuscripts in the British Museum,* I (1883), 890.

43. The Carole of the God of Love

Tho myghtist thou karoles sen,
And folk daunce and mery ben. . . .
There myghtist thou see these flowtours,
Mynstrales, and eke jogelours.

> *Romaunt of the Rose,* 759f., 763f.

. . . lowde mynstralcies
In cornemuse and shalemyes.

> *House of Fame,* 1217f.

Miniature in MS Bibl. Royale, Brussels, 11187, fol. 1. *Roman de la Rose.* Date ca. 1360. See E. Langlois, *Les Manuscrits du "Roman de la Rose"* (Paris, Lille, 1910), pp. 169, 172. The artist depicts, from left to right, minstrels playing a *shalemye* (shawm) and a *cornemuse* (bagpipe), Sweet-Looking with bow and arrow, Sir Mirth, Dame Gladness, the God of Love, crowned and winged, and four other dancers.

44. Opening Lines of Froissart's *Paradis Amoureus*

From MS Bibl. Nat. fr. 831, fol. 2. Date 1394. These lines Chaucer clearly imitated in the *Book of the Duchess*.

Chi commenche le Paradis Amoureus.

Je sui de moi en grant mervelle
Coument tant vifs, car moult je velle.
Et on ne poroit en vellant
Trouver de moi plus travellant.
Car bien sachies que par vellier
Me viennent souvent travellier
Pensees et merancolies,
Qui me sont ens ou cuer liies,
Et pas ne les pues desliier;
Car ne voel la belle oubliier
Pour quelle amour en ce travel
Je sui entres et tant je vel.

Et non pour quant ne pas lonch terme
Que de dormir euch voloir ferme,
Car tant priai a Morpheus,
A Juno, et a Oleus,
Qu'il m'envoiierent les messages
De dormir; je fis moult que sages,
Car se requis ne les euisse
Et fait a Juno sacrefisse
Seulement d'un anelet d'or,
Je croi que je villasse encor.
Mais la deesse noble et chiere
Tramist Yris sa messagiere
Pour moi au noble dieu dormant.

Here begins the *Paradise of Love*.

I am in a great wonder about myself,
How I live, for I am awake a great deal,
And one could not find anybody who suffers
More than I from sleeplessness.
For wit you well that through lack of sleep
There often come to trouble me
Thoughts and melancholy moods
Which are bound within my heart,
And I cannot unbind them;
For I do not wish to forget the fair lady
For love of whom I have entered
Into this sorrow and am so long wakeful.

And nevertheless, it is not a long time
Since I had a strong craving to sleep,
For I prayed so much to Morpheus,
To Juno, and to Oleus
That they would send me messengers
Of sleep. I did very wisely,

For if I had not asked them
And done sacrifice to Juno
Of only a little ring of gold,
I believe that I would be waking still.
But the noble and dear goddess
Sent Yris, her messenger,
On my behalf to the noble sleeping god.

Quod she to Juno, hir goddesse,
"Helpe me out of thys distresse,
And yeve me grace my lord to se
Soone, or wite wher-so he be. . . ."

Book of the Duchess, 106–12

Miniatures in ᴍs Bibl. Nat. fr. 1584. Machaut's
Dit de la Fontaine Amoureuse, decorated ca. 1370.
Fol. 157v. On the left is the love-sick poet. On the
right Alcione kneels before Juno, unconscious of
the body of Ceyx, drowned in the sea.

45–47. Ceyx and Alcione

. . . doun on knees she sat anoon
And wepte that pittee was to here.
"A! mercy! swete lady dere!"

This messager tok leve and wente
Upon hys wey, and never ne stente
Til he com to the derke valeye

That stant betwixen roches tweye. . . .
This messager com fleynge faste
And cried, "O, ho! awake anoon!"

Book of the Duchess, 153–56, 178f.

Fol. 158. On the left Iris is shown, winged and
partly wrapped in cloud, flying toward the walled
home of the god of sleep. On the upper right of
the page Iris flies into the house of the god, which
stands between two cliffs with a stream running
by, and finds him sleeping on a rich bed. At the
lower right is the drowsy poet.

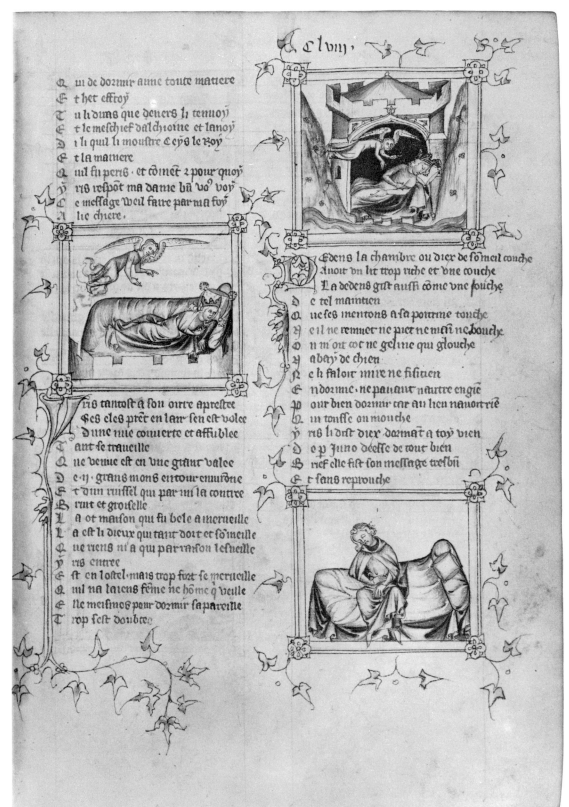

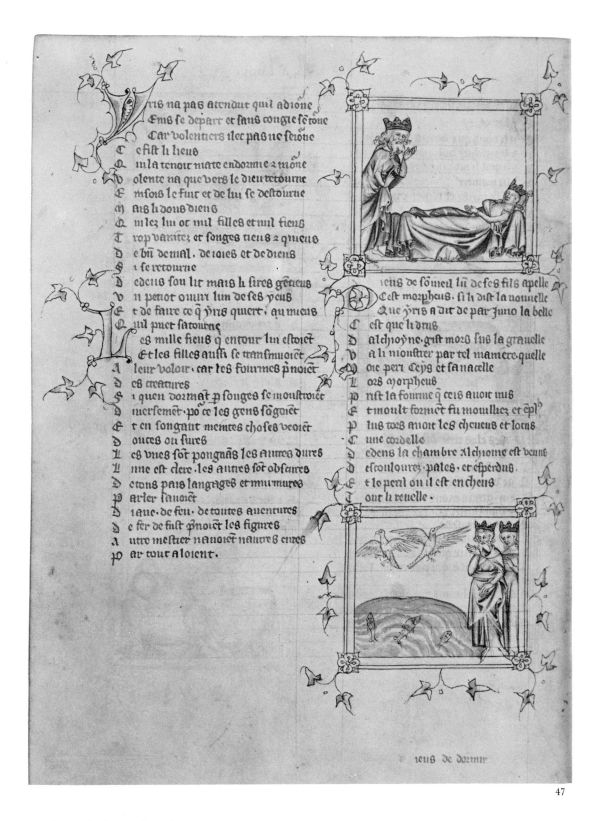

47

Anoon this god of slep abrayd
Out of hys slep, and gan to goon . . . ;
Took up the dreynte body sone
And bar hyt forth to Alcione, . . .
And stood ryght at hyr beddes fet.

Book of the Duchess, 192f., 195f., 199

Fol. 158v. In the upper miniature, Morpheus, who according to Machaut was a son of the god of sleep, appears to Alcione in the form of her drowned husband. Below we see Ceyx and Alcione transformed into the sea birds, not mentioned by Chaucer.

48. Uncoupling the Hounds

The mayster-hunte anoon, fot-hot,
With a gret horn blew thre mot
At the uncouplynge of hys houndes.
Withynne a while the hert yfounde ys,
Yhalowed, and rechased faste.

Book of the Duchess, 375–79

Miniature in MS Bibl. Nat. fr. 619, fol. 57. Gaston

Phébus, *Livre de la Chasse*. Date end of fourteenth century. The rubric reads: "Ci devise comment on doit aler lesser courre pour le cerf." ("Here it tells how one ought to go about letting [the hounds] run for the hart.") We see the master huntsman sounding his horn and the hounds pursuing a hart. Below, other huntsmen are removing the collars of other hounds. For another hunting scene see Fig. 152.

49, 50. The Phoenix

"Trewly she was, to myn ẏe,
The soleyn fenix of Arabẏe. . . ."

Book of the Duchess, 981f.

Miniatures from a bestiary, dated about 1300, in the University of Aberdeen Library, fols. 55v, 56. The phoenix was one of the best known of the fabulous creatures of the Middle Ages, and was depicted in numerous bestiaries. It was distinguished for its beauty and its uniqueness. Hence the compliment implied by the comparison of the Duchess Blanche with the bird. Only one of the species ever existed, and it renewed itself every 500 years. At the end of the period it collected twigs of spice plants, turned its body to the rays of the sun, and was consumed by the burning spices. But on the ninth day it rose again from the ashes. Fig. 49 shows the phoenix biting off the tendril of a spice plant, and Fig. 50 shows the bird in its nest, ignited by the sun.

49

50

51. Richmond Castle, Yorkshire

A long castel with walles white,
Be seynt Johan! on a ryche hil.

Book of the Duchess, 1318f.

A distant view of Richmond Castle, painted by J. M. W. Turner, now in the Fitzwilliam Museum, Cambridge. In the lines quoted above Chaucer combined the first name of John of Gaunt, who is the Man in Black of the poem, and his two titles, Duke of Lancaster (long castle) and Earl of Rich-mond (rich hill). See Tupper in *Modern Language Notes,* xxxi (1918), 250–52. If Chaucer ever saw Richmond Castle, it was probably when he was about fifteen years old and was visiting Yorkshire in the household of Prince Lionel. Turner's romantic vision would seem, accordingly, to correspond more closely to what the young poet envisaged than a modern photograph of the ruins.

51

52. Jupiter and Ganymede

"I neyther am Ennok, ne Elye,
Ne Romulus, ne Ganymede,
That was ybore up, as men rede,
To hevene with daun Jupiter,
And mad the goddys botiller."

House of Fame, 588–92

Miniature in MS Bibl. Nat. fr. 373, fol. 247, a manuscript (dated ca. 1400) of the *Ovide Moralisé,* which belonged to Jean Duc de Berry, the bibliophile and patron of the arts. Jupiter is seated on a rainbow, a large feather (?) in his right hand, and flakes of fire dropping from his left on five prostrate knights. Above, clouds are represented by a scallop pattern, and to the right, Jupiter in the form of an eagle bears up Ganymede in his talons. For the literary source of this composition see Wilkins in *Speculum,* XXXII (1957), 515f.

52

53. Alexander the Great as Aeronaut

"... half so high as this
Nas Alixandre Macedo,
Ne the kyng, Daun Scipio."

House of Fame, 914–16

Miniature in MS Berlin, Kupferstichkabinett 78. C. 1, fol. 66. Date ca. 1300. Alexander the Great is depicted holding aloft a baited spear in a cabin supported by flying gryphons. In their efforts to reach the bait they carry him higher and higher until the heat of the sun obliges him to turn the spear down and descend. Below are the wise men of Greece, gazing up at him. The rubric reads: "Coument Alixandres se fist porter en l'air as oyseals que len apele grif." ("How Alexander caused himself to be borne into the sky by birds which one calls 'gryphon.'") For other illustrations of this exploit see *Burlington Magazine,* VI (1905), 395–401; XXXII (1918), 136–40, 177–85.

53

54. Daedalus and Icarus

"Ne eke the wrechche Dedalus,
Ne his child, nyce Ykarus,
That fleigh so highe that the hete
Hys wynges malt, and he fel wete
In myd the see, and ther he dreynte."

House of Fame 919–23

Miniature in MS Lyon, Bibl. Mun. 142, fol. 138.
Ovide Moralisé. Date ca. 1380.

54

55. Architectural Details

Babewynnes and pynacles,
Ymageries and tabernacles,
I say, and ful eke of wyndowes.

House of Fame, 1189–91

External details of the hall and the muniment tower of New College, Oxford, built between 1380 and 1386, showing grotesque heads (*babewynnes*), pinnacles, and canopied niches (*tabernacles*) containing images of the Virgin, an angel, and the founder of the college, Bishop William of Wykeham. The bishop's crozier is shown in Fig. 37.

55

56

56. A Cannon and a Catapult

As swifte as pelet out of gonne,
When fyr is in the poudre ronne.

House of Fame, 1643f.

With grysely soun out goth the grete gonne.

Legend of Good Women, 637

And the noyse which that I herde,
For al the world, ryght so it ferde,
As dooth the rowtynge of the ston
That from th'engyn ys leten gon.

House of Fame, 1931–34

Miniature in Bodleian Library, Bodley 264, fol. 255. Date ca. 1410. English workmanship, illustrating Marco Polo's account of the siege of Saranfu in China. On the right is a catapult (*engyn*), prepared to hurl a stone at the wall. Next to it is one of the earliest pictures of a cannon (*gonne*), with a ball (*pelet*) in the mouth. It is being fired by a crouching "engineer," while a helmeted soldier stands at his side covering him with a large shield.

57. The Dream of Scipio

Fyrst telleth it, whan Scipion was come
In Affrike, how he meteth Massynisse,
That hym for joie in armes hath inome . . .
And how his auncestre, Affrycan so deere,
Gan in his slep that nyght to hym apere.
Thanne telleth it that, from a sterry place,
How Affrycan hath hym Cartage shewed . . .
. . . and shewede hym the Galaxye.
Thanne shewede he hym the lytel erthe that
here is . . .
And after shewede he hym the nyne speres.

Parliament of Fowls, 36–44, 56–59

Miniature in MS Bodleian Library, Can. Class lat.

257, fol. lv. *Somnium Scipionis* of Macrobius, Italian, date 1383. To the left of the circle representing the earth, Scipio Africanus Minor (185–129 B.C.) is embraced by Masinissa, King of Numidia. At the bottom, he lies in bed dreaming. At the top, he and Masinissa are joined in the dream by Scipio Africanus Major (234?–183 B.C.). To the right of the circle, the elder Scipio points to the earth, Terra, on which the cities of Roma and Cartago appear. The white band filled with stars is the Milky Way (Lactea Via), also called the Galaxy. The earth is enclosed successively by the spheres of Luna, Mercury, Venus, Sol, Mars, Jove, Saturn (unnamed), the Fixed Stars, and the Primum Mobile.

FORTUNE

58. The Poet, Fortune,
    and Her Wheel

FORTUNE: Thou born art in my regne of
            variaunce,
          Aboute the wheel with other most
            thou dryve. . . .
PLEINTIF: My frend maystow nat reven,
            blind goddesse.

Fortune, 45f., 50

Miniature in MS Bibl. Nat. fr. 1586, fol. 30v. Machaut's poems, dated ca. 1360. The upper part shows a poet, sitting in a walled wood beside a spring, composing his complaint to Fortune. Below, blindfolded Fortune operates her wheel by a crank and gear. At the top of the wheel is a crowned king, while one figure rises and another falls. On the subject see H. R. Patch, *The Goddess Fortuna* (Cambridge, Mass., 1927), pp. 147–77.

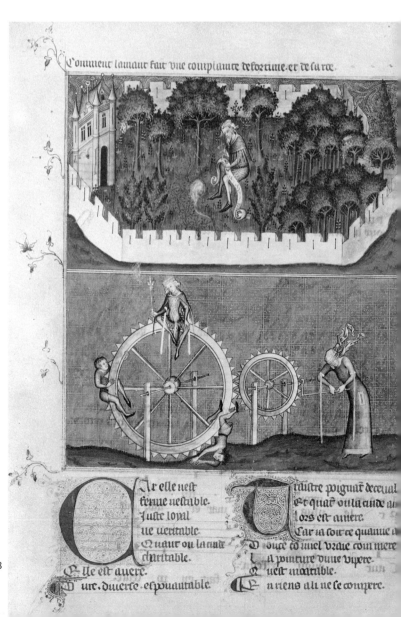

THE COMPLAINT OF MARS

59. Mars, Lord of Battle

But to yow, hardy knyghtes of renoun,
Syn that ye be of my devisioun. . . .

Complaint of Mars, 272f.

Miniature in MS British Museum Harley 4431,
fol. 101v. Christine de Pisan, *Epistre d'Othéa.* Date
ca. 1410. Mars is seated on a rainbow against a
starry background. Below are knights engaged in
combat.

60. Orpheus and Eurydice

The poete of Trace, that whilom hadde ryght greet sorwe for the deth of his wyf, . . . went hym to the houses of helle, and ther he tempride his blaundysschinge songes by resounynge strenges. . . . At the laste the lord and juge of soules was moevid to misericordes, and cryede: "We ben overcomen; . . . yyve we to Orpheus his wif to beren hym compaignye."

Boethius, III, metrum 12

Miniature in MS Bibl. Nat. fr. 871, fol. 196. *Ovide Moralisé*, dated ca. 1370. In the upper left we see the wedding of Orpheus and Eurydice, and winged Hymen hovering over them. To the right we see the death of Eurydice from the bite of a small dragon. Below, Orpheus appears, approaching the land of the shades, where Pluto and Persephone, with the shaggy bodies and claws of devils, reign, and where corpses are seen lying in their graves. On the lower left Eurydice follows Orpheus upward from Hades.

61

61. Orpheus Harping to the Birds and Beasts

The poete of Trace . . . hadde maked the hertes and the hyndes to joynen dreedles here sydes to cruel lyouns, and hadde maked that the hare was nat agast of the hound.

Boethius, III, metrum 12

Ther herde I pleyen on an harpe
That sowned bothe wel and sharpe,
Orpheus ful craftely.

House of Fame, 1201–03

Miniature in MS Bibl. Nat. fr. 871, fol. 196v. *Ovide Moralisé*, dated ca. 1370. Note, besides the birds, on Orpheus's right side a hart, a lion (?), and a dog; and on his left a horse (?), a unicorn, and a hare.

THE LEGEND OF
GOOD WOMEN

62. Ysoude

> "Hyde ye youre beautes, Ysoude and Eleyne,
> My lady cometh, that al this may disteyne."
>
> *Legend of Good Women*, F, 254f.

A water-color copy by L. Yperman of a mural painting in the castle of St. Floret, near Issoire, Puy-de-Dôme. Date ca. 1350. Ysoude (Isolt) is depicted pointing upward to the head of her husband, King Mark, who is spying on her and Tristan from a tree. Her chin and throat are covered by a white gorget, and she wears a sideless *côte-hardie*. See R. S. and L. H. Loomis, *Arthurian Legends in Medieval Art* (New York, London, 1938), pp. 57–59.

63. A Chest

> "Hastow nat in a book, lyth in thy cheste,
> The grete goodnesse of the quene Alceste?"
>
> *Legend of Good Women*, F, 510f.

A water-color painting of a chest, now in the Burrell Collection, Glasgow. Date of chest 1340–1367. The lid still preserves tempera paintings, which represent, from left to right, a lion rampant; two heraldic shields with arms of the d'Aungerville family; a wyvern encountering a half-man half-beast, equipped with sword and buckler; a shield with the leopards of England quartered with the lilies of France; the arms of Neville; a rampant wyvern. The chest, long in the Chancery Court,

62

Durham, was probably a repository of coin or official documents, under the custody of Richard d'Aungerville, Bishop of Durham, and Lord Neville. See Wells in *Connoisseur,* CLI (1962), 4.

63

64

64. Antony and Cleopatra

. . . Whan that Antony saw that aventure . . .
. . . for dispeyr out of his wit he sterte . . .
And rof hymself anon thourghout the herte. . . .
Among the serpents in the pit she sterte,
And there she ches to have hire buryinge.
Anon the nadderes gonne hire for to stynge.

Legend of Good Women, 657, 660f., 697–99

Miniature in MS Bibl. Nat. fr. 12420, fol. 129v.
A French translation of Boccaccio's *De Claris Mulieribus.* Date 1401.

66

67

65

65. Pyramus and Thisbe

And with that word his swerd she tok as swythe,
That warm was of hire loves blod, and hot,
And to the herte she hireselven smot.
And thus are Tisbe and Piramus ygo.

Legend of Good Women, 913–16

Miniature in MS Bibl. Nat. fr. 12420, fol. 20.
A French translation of Boccaccio's *De Claris Mulieribus.* Date 1401.

66. Jason at Colchis

Ther was swich tydyng overal and swich loos,
That in an yle that called was Colcos . . .
That therin was a ram, that men mighte se,
That hadde a fles of gold that shon so bryghte
That nowher was swich anothir syghte;
But it was kepte alwey with a dragoun, . . .
And with two boles, maked al of bras.

Legend of Good Women, 1424–32

Miniature in MS British Museum. Harley 4431,
fol. 120. Christine de Pisan, *Epistre d'Othéa la
Déesse.* Date ca. 1410. Jason has already killed
the bulls and is attacking the dragon. Above to
the left is the ram.

67. Jason Deserts Ypsiphile

The somme is this, that Jason wedded was, . . .
And upon hire begat he children two,
And drogh his sayl, and saw hir nevere mo.
A letter sente she to hym, certeyn, . . .
And hym reprevith of his grete untrouthe, . . .
And that she moste bothe hire chyldren spylle.

Legend of Good Women, 1559–74

Miniature in MS Bibl. Nat. fr. 12420, fol. 25.
A French translation of Boccaccio's *De Claris
Mulieribus.* Date 1401. Jason boards a ship, leaving Ypsiphile behind. Two helmed women prepare
to kill her children.

TROILUS AND CRISEYDE

68. Chaucer Reciting *Troilus* to the Court

Now herkneth with a good entencioun,
For now wil I gon streght to my matere,
In which ye may the double sorwes here

Of Troilus in lovynge of Criseyde,
And how that she forsook hym er she deyde.

Troilus, I, 52–56

Miniature in MS Corpus Christi College, Cambridge 61, fol. 1v. This is a luxury manuscript of *Troilus,* made a few years after Chaucer's death, perhaps for Joan Beaufort, John of Gaunt's daughter and the poet's niece, for it was later in the possession of Joan's daughter, Anne Neville. The splendid frontispiece shows Chaucer, apparently in his prime, reciting the poem to the royal circle in an outdoor setting. He is standing in a pulpit; immediately to his right is seated a man robed in cloth of gold, evidently King Richard. The latter's face has been badly rubbed, perhaps by some Lancastrian fanatic. The woman wearing a coronal at Richard's right is surely Queen Anne. The identification of other personages is a speculative matter, but Dr. Margaret Galway has made one suggestion which seems highly plausible, namely, that the matronly figure with coronal in the front row is the King's mother (widow of the Black Prince), Joan of Kent, of whom we have an earlier portrait in Fig. 20. See M. Galway in *Modern Language Review,* XLIV (1949), 161–77 (with colored reproduction); A. Brusendorff, *The Chaucer Tradition* (London, 1925), pp. 19–25. The parklike setting and the lofty towers are more decorative than realistic in treatment. The essential truth is that the poet must have read or recited his work to appreciative courtly audiences.

69

69. Troilus and Criseyde in the Temple

And to the temple, in al hir beste wise,
In general ther wente many a wight. . . .
Among thise othere folk was Criseyda. . . .
This Troilus, as he was wont to gide
His yonge knyghtes, lad hem up and down, . . .
Byholding ay the ladies of the town. . . .
She, this in blak, likynge to Troilus
Over alle thing, he stood for to biholde.

   Troilus, I, 162f., 169, 183f., 186, 309f.

Miniature in MS Florence, Bibl. Naz. II. II. 90, fol. 67. Boccaccio, *Filostrato,* dated ca. 1380. Criseyde is surely the lady clad in long mantle and hood on the left. Troilus is probably the right-hand figure of the three knights advancing toward the ladies, and he seems to be repeated at the extreme left.

70. Pandarus Visits Love-Sick Troilus

Bywaylyng in his chambre thus allone,
A frend of his, that called was Pandare,
Com oones in unwar, and herde hym groone,
And say his frend in swich destresse and care.

Troilus, I, 547–50

Miniature in MS Florence, Bibl. Naz. II. II. 90, fol. 68v. Boccaccio, *Filostrato,* dated ca. 1380. Note that according to Boccaccio Pandaro was a young man, and so he is represented here.

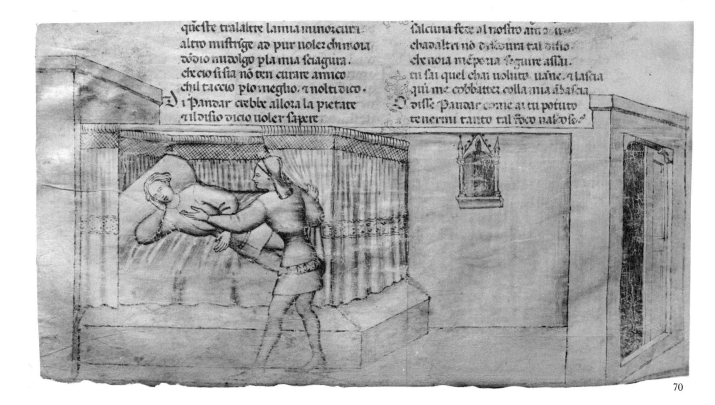

70

71. Hector of Troy

"Of Ector nedeth it namore for to telle:
In al this world ther nys a bettre knyght
Than he, that is of worthynesse welle."

Troilus, II, 176–78

A tapestry which originally began a series representing the Nine Worthies, the greatest warriors in history according to a list in a poem, *Les Voeux du Paon,* composed about 1312. The set of three tapestries was woven about 1400 for Jean Duc de Berry, the art lover and bibliophile. (See Figs. 25, 35, 52, 73, 102, 120, 124, 149.) Five of the nine figures have survived, though damaged, and are in the Cloisters Museum, New York. Hector is identified by the fact that he is the first of the three pagan warriors and by the device on his shield, a lion sitting on a chair. He is seated on a throne under a *tabernacle,* and four armed men appear in *tabernacles* on either side of him. On the Nine Worthies in art see R. S. and L. H. Loomis, *Arthurian Legends in Medieval Art* pp. 37–40, 140; R. L. Wyss in *Zeitschrift für schweizerische Archäologie und Kunstgeschichte,* XVII (1917), 73–106. On the tapestries at the Cloisters see J. J. Rorimer and M. Freeman, *Nine Heroes Tapestries at the Cloisters* (New York, 1953), which wrongly identifies this figure with Alexander.

71

72. Mount Helicon, Apollo, Pallas, the Muses, and Pegasus

Yee sustren nyne ek, that by Elicone
In hil Pernaso listen for t'abide.

Troilus, III, 1809f.

And ye, me to endite and ryme
Helpeth, that on Parnaso duelle,
Be Elicon, the clere welle.

House of Fame, 520–22

    Pallas, ful of grace,
Be present and my song contynue and guye....
Be favorable eke, thou Polymya,
On Parnaso that with thy sustres glade,
By Elycon, not fer from Cirrea,
Singest with vois memorial in the shade.

Anelida, 5f., 15–18

And seyden it was lyk the Pegasee,
The hors that hadde wynges for to flee.

Squire's Tale, 207f.

Me were looth be likned, doutelees,
To Muses that men clepe Pierides—
Metamorphosios woot what I mene.

Man of Law's Headlink, 91–93

Miniature in MS Bibl. Nat. fr. 871, fol. 116v. *Ovide Moralisé,* an allegorical interpretation of Ovid's *Metamorphoses.* Date ca. 1370. Apollo, with his harp, sits on one of the peaks of Mount Helicon, which Chaucer confused with Parnassus. At the god's feet is the spring started by the hoof of the winged horse Pegasus. In the pool, which Chaucer mistakenly called Elicon, the Nine Muses are bathing. Above them the daughters of Pierus, the Pierides, are perched in the form of magpies. At the right stands Pallas, crowned. On Chaucer's references to Elicon and Parnaso see Lowes in *Modern Philology,* XIV, 705–35.

73

73. Juno

"And blisful Juno, thorugh hire grete myght,
Shal, as I hope, hire grace unto us sende."

Troilus, IV, 1116f.

Miniature in MS Bibl. Nat. fr. 373, fol. 51. *Ovide Moralisé,* which belonged to Jean Duc de Berry. Date ca. 1400. As queen of the gods Juno stands holding a scepter, with conventionalized clouds and a rainbow above her head. On each side is a peacock, her sacred bird.

74. Rochester Castle and Bridge

"Loo, Rouchestre stant heer faste by!"
Monk's Prologue, 1926

An aquatint by Joseph Farington in Boydell's *History of the River Thames*. The most conspicuous feature of medieval Rochester, as it still is today, was the main tower of the castle, built 1126–1139, rising to a height of 120 feet. The bridge over the River Medway, shown in the picture, was built in 1383 under the supervision of the great architect Henry Yevele, who was associated with Chaucer when the latter was Clerk of the King's Works. It was over this bridge that the Pilgrims would have approached Rochester. See John Harvey, *Henry Yevele* (London, 1944), p. 59.

75. The West Gate, Canterbury

The west gate of the walled town of Canterbury, through which the Pilgrims would have entered, was built under the direction of Chaucer's associate, Yevele, in 1378. See John Harvey, *Henry Yevele,* p. 61. The print shows the gate as it was in the middle of the nineteenth century, when the wall had been removed. The houses outside the gate probably belong to the sixteenth or seventeenth century. T. Dugdale, *Curiosities of Great Britain, England and Wales Delineated* (London, 1854–60), Vol. II.

76. An Inn at Canterbury

No medieval picture of the Tabard Inn, South-

wark, where the Pilgrims assembled, has been preserved. However, we have an old print showing a hostelry where, according to a lively fifteenth-century continuation of the *Tales,* Harry Bailey and his flock were accommodated on their arrival at Canterbury. See R. S. Loomis, R. Willard, *Medieval English Verse and Prose* (New York, 1948), pp. 373–78; A. P. Stanley, *Historical Memorials of Canterbury,* Everyman's Library, pp. 217f., 232f. The original inn stood on the corner of High Street and Mercery Lane, close to the Cathedral. It was called the Chequer of the Hope, possibly referring to a sign (not shown in the print) consisting of a chessboard and a barrel hoop, advertising the games and beverages available to patrons.

77. Murder in the Cathedral

Miniature in MS British Museum Harley 5102, fol. 32. A psalter, produced possibly as early as 1173, the date of St. Thomas's canonization, since after that date he would be represented with a halo. Chaucer must have seen numerous depictions of the sensational murder of the archbishop in his cathedral, and some of them might have been executed as soon after the event of 1170 as this miniature. The dark interior is lighted by a lamp suspended from the arch. The pontiff is falling toward the altar, as Fitzurse, identified by the bear painted on his shield, strikes at his head, knocking off his cap. Tracy slashes at the arm of a monk named Grim, holding a crozier, who tries to shield the victim. Le Bret is depicted with a pointless sword to indicate that when he struck the fatal blow at the prostrate form, he broke his blade on the pavement. It must be Moreville whose unarmed head and sword appear on the left, for he, though present, took no part in the attack. For an account of the murder see A. P. Stanley, *Historical Memorials of Canterbury,* Everyman's Library, pp. 69–93. On the miniature see T. Borenius, *St. Thomas Becket in Art* (London, 1932), p. 92; pl. XXXVII, 1.

78. Henry II Doing Penance at the Shrine of St. Thomas

A stained-glass panel in the Bodleian Library, Oxford, dating probably from the middle of the fifteenth century. The shrine of the martyr (see Fig. 79) is seen in the upper left corner, though it did not exist in 1174, when Henry II, acknowledging himself to be the unwitting cause of the murder of the archbishop, submitted to scourging by bishops, abbots, and monks as a sign of penitence. See Stanley, *Historical Memorials of Canterbury,* Everyman's Library, pp. 116–18, 120 n. 3; pp. 224–29. For the glass panel see John Carter, *Specimens of Ancient Sculpture and Painting* (1780), pl. 37; pp. 50–52; J. A. Knowles in *Bodleian Quarterly Record,* v (1926–28), 100–04.

79. A Vision of St. Thomas and His Shrine

A stained-glass panel, dated about 1220, in Canterbury Cathedral depicts an unnamed monk asleep on a couch. He sees in a vision the martyred archbishop, in full pontificals, emerging from his shrine and bending over him. It was this shrine, glittering with jewels of incalculable value donated by merchants, princes, and kings, which was for most pilgrims the high point of a visit to Canterbury. Concealed within it was an iron chest containing the saint's body. Here the pilgrims recited their prayers, and the diseased were allowed to rub their limbs against the marble base. On the subject of the shrine see A. P. Stanley, *Historical Memorials of Canterbury,* Everyman's Library, pp. 226–29, 237–40. On the glass see B. Rackham, *Ancient Glass of Canterbury Cathedral* (London, 1949), p. 91; pl. xii (opposite p. 98).

THE CANTERBURY PILGRIMS

Three manuscripts of the *Canterbury Tales* contain, or once contained, miniatures representing the tellers of the tales on horseback, each at the point where he or she begins the tale. Of these manuscripts two are fragmentary and are dated between 1440 and 1460. Worse than that, the decorators of these two manuscripts paid little or no attention to Chaucer's descriptions in the General Prologue, with the result that they frequently misrepresented the physical features or the attire of the Pilgrims, added details which did not belong, or omitted details which the poet mentioned. The decorator of MS Cambridge University Library Gg. IV. 27 drew horses of such a peculiar anatomy and with such vicious eyes as to give the effect of caricature to all his figures. Since such illustrations defeat the purpose of this book, which is to help the beholder to see, as far as possible, what Chaucer wanted him to see, this manuscript and the other defective manuscript, now divided between the Rosenbach Foundation in Philadelphia and the John Rylands Library in Manchester, have not been drawn on to furnish portraits of the Pilgrims. Those, however, who are curious to discover how far the distorting lenses of the mid-fifteenth century could misrepresent Chaucer's conceptions may find the miniatures of the Cambridge manuscript reproduced in Chaucer Society *Publications,* 1st ser., XCVI, Part II, and described in terms of artistic technique by Margaret Rickert in *The Text of the "Canterbury Tales,"* ed. J. M. Manly, E. Rickert (Chicago, 1940), I, 590–93, 596–604. They may also find the Miller of the Rylands Library manuscript reproduced in the *Bulletin* of the Library, XVII (1933), 346, and likewise described by M. Rickert, *loc. cit.,* I, 571, 590–92, and the Cook of the Rosenbach manuscript reproduced in *An Exhibition of Fifteenth Century Manuscripts and Books in Honor of the Six Hundredth Anniversary of the Birth of Geoffrey Chaucer* (Rosenbach Company, New York, 1940), frontispiece.

Far superior as illustration of Chaucer's text is the complete set of miniatures of the tellers of the tales in the Ellesmere manuscript, which formerly belonged to the Earl of Ellesmere and is now preserved in the Henry E. Huntington Library at San Marino, California. The manuscript, which is noted for the excellence of its text, has been reproduced in facsimile (Manchester, 1911). Margaret Rickert furnished a technical description of the miniatures, *loc. cit.,* I, 590–93, 596–604. They have been reproduced and spiritedly described by E. F. Piper in *Philological Quarterly,* III (1924), 241–56.

The decoration of the Ellesmere manuscript was carried out by at least two artists, one of them distinguished by his placing the riders on small plots of grass. They inserted the figures in the margins opposite the beginning of the tale to be told, as noted above, and not opposite the description in the General Prologue. But, unlike the later miniaturists whose work has been excluded from this book, they read and followed with some fidelity the poet's descriptions; and, since they performed their task within ten years of his death, there was hardly time for anachronism in costume and other *realia* to creep in. In order to facilitate comparison with the descriptions in the Prologue, I have arranged the miniatures, not in the order of their occurrence in the Ellesmere manuscript, but in the order of the Prologue. For Chaucer's own conception of the Pilgrims see Muriel Bowden, *A Commentary on the General Prologue to the "Canterbury Tales"* (New York, 1948).

80. The Knight

Chaucer described the Knight as "late ycome from his viage," and apparently still wearing military costume, such as we see on the effigy of the Black Prince at Canterbury (Fig. 19). The *gypon,* a tight-fitting tunic of coarse stuff, covered

the *habergeon,* a short coat of mail reaching to the hips. See Herben in *Speculum,* XII (1937), 477–80. The miniaturist substituted for the *gypon* an apparently padded, knee-length gown with wide sleeves and close-fitting cuffs. The horse is a sturdy animal, and seems to have been branded on the flank with the letter *M.* See Manly and Rickert, I, 149; Piper in *Philological Quarterly,* III, 242.

81. The Squire

The Squire is depicted in spirited fashion and in agreement with Chaucer's description. His locks are frizzed. His short green gown is embroidered with white and red flowers, and the sleeves are wide and long. He sits easily on his curvetting palfrey. See Piper in *Philological Quarterly,* III, 247f.

82. The Prioress

The Prioress is riding sidesaddle. Her habit is Benedictine, as was the nunnery of Bromley from which she came; she wears a black cloak over a white tunic, and a white barb covers the throat and chin. In accordance with the text, her mouth is small, her forehead broad, and coral beads adorn her left wrist. See Piper in *Philological Quarterly,* III, 249.

81

83. The Second Nun

Chaucer tells us nothing about the nun who accompanied the Prioress as her chaplain, and the tale which he assigned to her was originally intended for a man. Accordingly, for a character

83

so little individualized it is natural that the miniaturist merely repeated his image of the Prioress, with the sole alteration of reversing her seat on the horse, so that she faces to the left instead of the right. Her face has a cherubic innocence. See Piper in *Philological Quarterly,* III, 253.

84. The Nun's Priest

In the General Prologue not a word is said about the appearance of the three priests who accompanied the Prioress, but later the Host picks out one of them and gives us to understand that his mount was a lean jade, but that the Priest himself was a brawny, large-chested, masculine type, with the eyes of a hawk and a ruddy skin. The artist seems not to have heeded these specifications except that the mount might pass for a jade. The man himself is not burly, and his face is pale and almost effeminate. In accordance with pre-Elizabethan custom he wears the red gown of a priest. See Piper in *Philological Quarterly,* III, 253.

85. The Monk

The Monk, a full-faced, corpulent figure, is dressed in a black habit and wide-brimmed hat. Two details mentioned in the text the artist has ignored, the gray fur trimmings at the wrists and the gold pin which fastens the Monk's hood, and the hat prevents our seeing his shiny bald pate. The harness of his palfrey jingles with many gold bells, and two greyhounds (not reproduced) gambol about him. See Piper in *Philological Quarterly,* III, 252.

86. The Friar

This miniature is one of the least satisfactory of the Ellesmere gallery. To be sure, we have a man of stout build in the habit of a friar, and may detect a twinkle in his eye. But beyond this the correspondence does not go. There is no tippet or semicope visible, and surely the figure does not possess the air of authority and charm which Chaucer attributes to the Friar. See Piper in *Philological Quarterly,* III, 245. See also Figs. 107, 108, 150.

87. The Merchant

On his cantering steed and with outflung arm, the Merchant seems a more dashing figure than in Chaucer's description, and his forked beard is conspicuous by its absence. But he sits "high on horse," his red gown with blue and white flowers represents *mottelee,* and we may assume that his hat with the roll brim is in the Flaundrish style. See Piper in *Philological Quarterly,* III, 247.

87

88

88. The Clerk of Oxenford

This is among the least satisfying of the Ellesmere portrayals. For, though the Clerk's mount is as lean as a rake, its ribs showing plainly, the man himself seems to be far from hollow, and his receding forehead hardly suggests an intellectual type devoted to Aristotle and his philosophy. However, his bookishness is to be inferred from the two volumes clutched under his threadbare *courtepy* and from a third volume held out in his right hand. See Piper in *Philological Quarterly,* III, 246.

89. The Sergeant of the Law

The lawyer wears the "medlee cote" which Chaucer assigned to him, half blue, half red, but the girdle of silk with narrow bars is missing. A cape covers his shoulders, and his head is covered by the coif which denotes his profession and his rank as a judge. See Fig. 31, and Piper in *Philological Quarterly,* III, 244.

89

90

indulgence in the pleasures of the cuisine. In fact, the artist has depicted the kind of man whom Chaucer described and who would tell the Franklin's Tale. See Piper in *Philological Quarterly*, III, 248.

91. The Cook

The drunken Cook is one of the most skillfully portrayed of all the Pilgrims. The face is that of a somewhat befuddled exhibitionist. He waves his cap with one hand and a flesh hook, the sign of his occupation, with the other, as he sits unsteadily on a rude pad. His legs are bare except for the bandage which covers the *mormal* on his shin. The horse turns his head around in disgusted curiosity to see what kind of fool he has on his back. See Piper in *Philological Quarterly,* III, 243f.

92. The Shipman

The Shipman is depicted very much as the poet described him—bearded, clad in a dark gown falling below the knee, a dagger slung under his arm from a red band over his left shoulder. His face is that of a ruffian. See Piper in *Philological Quarterly*, III, 249.

90. The Franklin

The Franklin rides a softly stepping horse. His hair and beard are white as a daisy. A *gipser* (see Fig. 111) hangs from his girdle. There is no evidence that his waistline suffers from over-

91

92

93

94

93. The Doctor of Physic

The miniaturist has conscientiously followed the indications of the text as to coloring of the Physician's costume, a blood-red (*sangwyn*) gown, a hood and attached cape of *pers* (slate-blue). Unmentioned by the poet and, of course, quite unrealistic as a pose taken by the mounted Pilgrim is the examination of a urinal. This object is introduced merely as a sign of the latter's profession. See Fig. 113; the Host's endlink to the Physician's Tale, 305; Piper in *Philological Quarterly*, III, 248.

94. The Wife of Bath

In depicting the Wife of Bath the illustrator has faithfully reproduced the chief details of her description—the wide-brimmed hat, the foot-mantle about her large hips, the spurs with rowels. But instead of a wimple about her hair and neck, she wears a gold net. Unlike the nuns, she rides astride, and her *amblere* is really ambling, lifting the legs on the far side together. See Piper in *Philological Quarterly*, III, 245.

95. The Parson

Perhaps the most disappointing miniature in the Ellesmere gallery is that of the Parson. Like the Nun's Priest, he wears the red garb then customary

in his profession, and the scantiness of his horse furniture and the hands crossed over his chest may have been intended as evidences of his exemplary piety. But the squat figure and the crude features counteract that worthy intention. See Piper in *Philological Quarterly*, III, 254.

95

96. The Miller

The artist has succeeded in making the Miller a most repulsive hulk of a man, big of brawn and bones, riding a sullen plug and hunched over his bagpipe, with which, as Chaucer says, he played the Pilgrims out of town. Here, too, are the sword and buckler and the thumb of gold—in fact, two thumbs, both liberally gilded. A slightly later glossator made sure of the Miller's identity by the inscription "Robin with his Bagpype." See Piper in *Philological Quarterly*, III, 242f.

97. The Manciple

Since Chaucer provided no description of the Manciple's physique and his attire, the miniaturist was free to represent him as he pleased, with a smart mustache and pointed beard, a red cap, a blue gown lined with red, a white girdle, and red hose. From the pouch at his waist the Manciple has drawn a small gourd filled with wine, and offers it to the already drunken Cook. See Piper in *Philological Quarterly*, III, 244.

98. The Reeve

In accordance with the poet's description, the Reeve is depicted as a slender, long-legged, smooth-shaven type, mounted on a dapple-gray animal. The blue coat and the formidable sword also derive from the text, and to these details the artist has added a pair of keys, dangling from the girdle. See Piper in *Philological Quarterly*, III, 243.

99

100

99. The Summoner

The artist has not done full justice to Chaucer's horrendous portrait of the Summoner. Only the "scalled browes," the "piled berd," and the face, red as that of a cherub in medieval art, carry out the disgusting impression conveyed by the poet. A garland crowns the scoundrel's head as in the text, but the buckler made of a cake is missing. He is provided with a riding crop or wand, a sword at his side, and a summons in his right hand. See Piper in *Philological Quarterly*, III, 245f.

100. The Pardoner

Evidently the Pardoner struck the artist's imagination, for here are the cap with *vernicle* sewed onto it, the hanks of yellow hair spreading over the shoulders, the smooth chin, and the brass cross set with stones—all in conformity with the text. The wallet all brimful of pardons has, however, been shifted from the Pardoner's lap and slung round the horse's neck, where it would not cramp the rider's style. See Piper in *Philological Quarterly*, III, 248f.

101. The Canon's Yeoman

Lacking any instructions from the text as to the appearance of the Canon's servant, the miniaturist contented himself with depicting him in a red hat,

green jacket with wide sleeves, and red hose, indicating, however, the fellow's shabby estate by a white patch on the knee and a wisp of hair peeping through a hole in his hat. See Piper in *Philological Quarterly*, III, 253f.

THE GENERAL PROLOGUE OF THE *CANTERBURY TALES*

102. The Sun in April

Whan that Aprill with his shoures soote
The droghte of March hath perced to the roote,
. . . and the yonge sonne
Hath in the Ram his halve cours yronne . . . .

General Prologue, lf., 7f.

Detail of a miniature in the magnificent Book of
Hours at the Musée Condé, Chantilly, known as
the *Trés Riches Heures* of Jean Duc de Berry and
dated 1409–1415. On the calendar page assigned
to the month of April we see, depicted against a
spring landscape, a courtier exchanging rings with
his ladylove, and two ladies picking flowers. Above
in a semicircular frame are represented the sun in
his chariot; a band divided into thirty parts cor-
responding to the days of the month; and another
band showing the starry sky, the first part of which,
up to the twelfth day, is the second half-course of
the Ram, and the rest of which is occupied by the
zodiacal sign of the Bull.

103. The Capture of Alexandria

At Alisaundre he was whan it was wonne.

General Prologue (Knight), 51

Miniature in MS Bibl. Nat., fr. 1584, fol. 309.
Machaut, *Prise d'Alexandrie*. The date of the miniature is not more than fifteen years after the capture
of Alexandria from the Turks in 1365 by an
amphibious landing of Crusaders commanded by
King Peter of Cyprus. It is possible that Chaucer
saw the King when he was a guest of Edward III
at Westminster and Windsor in 1363. A stanza in
the Monk's Tale is devoted to King Peter's tragic
fate. Chaucer credits the Knight with taking part
in the capture of the city. See Muriel Bowden, *A
Commentary on the General Prologue to the "Canterbury
Tales"* (New York, 1948), pp. 60–62.

Cy commence le liure de
la prise dalyxandre

Quant li dieu pamos amoient
Et les deesses se renouoient
Aus dous gieus courtois sauours
Qi sot fais pour les amoureus
Clers solaus la belle lune
Et des estoiles la commune
Li ciij. signe et les planettes
Qui sot clers luisans et nettes
Esdenerent j. parlement
Par deu munn assentement
La or mainte dieu de grant puissance
Et digne de grant reuerence
Et maintes deesses aussi
Ne ie ne nomeray pas ci
Car trop longue chose seroit
Qui tous et toutes nommeroit
Nymphes de bois et de riuieres
Autreslus de toutes manieres
Les tragedianes y vindrent
Qui mult humblement se contindrent
Tragedianes sacrefice
Font aus dieu et deum office
Et nymphes en poetarie
Ce sont fees ie ne doubtmie

Mars ne fu pas a lassamblee
Pour bien estoit assamblee
Mre la male enchanteresse
Car elle eust tout empeeschie
Qot ce eust este grant peschie
Venus sert par especial
A ceste assamblee roial
Mais qui est li dieus de bataille
Et la bentis sans faille
Ce si estoit pas oubliee
Mais estoit vestue et paree
Com deesse royne et dame
Ancops en bies en cuer en ame
Et tous ceaus qui pamours aiment
Onre et p dieu de ceaus qui naiment
Car homs ne li puet eschaper
Mis quelle le demeine attraper
Mars leur dist tout en audience
Ie say que chascuns de vous pesce
I bon et chier amy soit mort
Et fine p piteuse mort
Ce sont li bon roy alixandres
Qui conquist anglestre et flandres

104. Archers

A Yeman hadde he and servantz namo. . . .
A sheef of pecock arwes, bright and kene
Under his belt he bar ful thriftily . . .
And in his hand he baar a myghty bowe. . . .
Upon his arm he baar a gay bracer.

General Prologue (Yeoman), 101–11

Miniature in margin of Luttrell Psalter, British Museum Add. 42130, fol. 147v. East Anglian manuscript, dated ca. 1340. A group of men practicing archery. The instructor and one of the group are shown wearing *bracers* (arm guards) on their left forearms. See E. G. Millar, *Luttrell Psalter* (London, 1932), p. 38.

105. Nuns in Choir

Ful weel she soong the service dyvyne
Entuned in hir nose ful semely.

General Prologue (Prioress), 122f.

Page in MS British Museum Domitian A XVII, fol. 177v. Psalter of King Henry VI, probably made in Paris ca. 1430. See G. F. Warner, *Illuminated Manuscripts in the British Museum* (London, 1903); and *British Museum, Schools of Illumination*, VI (1930), 10.

106. A Crowned *A*

And theron heng a brooch of gold ful sheene,
On which ther was first write a crowned A.
General Prologue (Prioress), 160f.

A leaden ornament in the Guildhall Museum,
London, No. 8731. The letters *M* and *A*, standing
for Maria (the Virgin Mary), are combined to
form a single letter surmounted by a crown.

106

107

107. Friars Entertained at High Table

A lymytour, a ful solemne man. . . .
Ful wel biloved and famulier was he
With frankeleyns over al in his contree.
General Prologue (Friar), 209, 215f.

Miniature in the Luttrell Psalter, British Museum
Add. 42130, fol. 208. East Anglian manuscript
dated ca. 1340. A man of property, perhaps a
franklin, and his wife entertain two Dominican
friars and three other guests at a trestle table. Two
servants wait on the company. See E. G. Millar,
Luttrell Psalter (London, 1932), p. 49.

108

108. A Friar Hearing Confession

Ful swetely herde he confessioun,
And plesaunt was his absolucioun.
General Prologue (Friar), 221f.

Miniature in the Luttrell Psalter, British Museum
Add. 42130, fol. 74. East Anglian manuscript
dated ca. 1340. A Franciscan friar listens to the
confession of a nun. See E. G. Millar, *Luttrell Psalter*
(London 1932), p. 31.

109. Aristotle

For hym was levere have at his beddes heed
Twenty bookes, clad in blak or reed,
Of Aristotle and his philosophie,
Than robes riche or fithele or gay sautrie.

General Prologue (Clerk), 293–96

Miniature in Columbia University Library, Plimpton Collection, MS 7, fol. 3. Walter Burley's translation of Aristotle's *Nichomachean Ethics* into Latin, dated 1391. For *fithele* and *sautrye* see Fig. 164.

109

110

110. A Fishpond

Ful many a fat partrich hadde he in muwe,
And many a breem and many a luce in stuwe.

General Prologue (Franklin), 349f.

Wall painting by Matteo di Giovanetti da Viterbo in the palace of the Popes at Avignon. Date of painting 1343–1350. See *Gazette des Beaux-Arts,* LVI (1914), 2nd sem., 293–316. From left to right around the fishpond we see four men, one stooping, one examining the fish in his net, one about to cast in his net (?), and one with a hawk on his fist. Pools for the breeding of fish supplied much of the most delicious food for the table, especially on fast days.

111. A *Gipser*

A gipser al of silk
Heeng at his girdel.

General Prologue (Franklin), 357f.

A pouch (fourteenth century) at the Musée de Cluny, Paris, embroidered in colored silks with designs of hybrid creatures, half human, half horse.

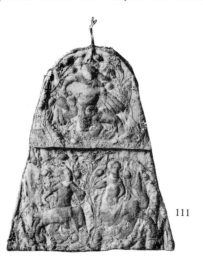

111

112. The Zodiacal Man

> With us ther was a Doctour of Phisik:
> In al this world ne was ther noon hym lik,
> To speke of phisik and of surgerye,
> For he was grounded in astronomye.
>
> General Prologue, 411–14

Wellcome MS in Historical Medical Museum, London, fol. 41. Date fifteenth century. The illustration shows the relation between the parts of the body, the signs of the zodiac, and the celestial luminaries. See O. Kurz, *Medical Illustrations of the Wellcome Manuscript;* H. Bober in *Journal of the Warburg and Courtauld Institutes,* XI (1948), 1–26.

113. Aesculapius and Circe

> With us ther was a Doctour of Phisik . . .
> Wel knew he the olde Esculapius.
>
> General Prologue, 411, 429

113

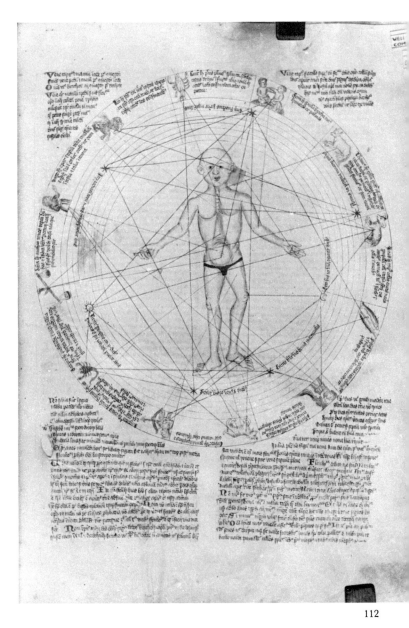

112

Th'enchauntementz of Medea and Circes.
Knight's Tale, 1944

Miniature in MS British Museum Harley 4431, fol. 113. Christine de Pisan, *Epistre d'Othéa la Déesse.* Date 1410–1415. Aesculapius, the traditional father of medicine, is examining a glass urinal (as the Physician does in Fig. 93) while a patient stands beside him. Circe, who worked cures by enchantment, is catching frogs for that purpose. On the miniatures in the Harley manuscript see L. Schaefer in *Jahrbuch für Kunstwissenschaft,* X (1937), 119–35, 162f.

114. Marriage at the Church Door

A good Wif was ther of biside Bathe....
Housbondes at chirche dore she hadde fyve.

General Prologue, 445, 460

But finally ycomen is the day
That to the chirche bothe be they went
For to receyve the hooly sacrament.
Forth comth the preest, with stole about his nekke.

Merchant's Tale, 1700–03

Miniature in MS Bodleian Library, Bodley 264, fol. 105. French *Alexander,* made at Bruges. Date

1338–1344. The bride is being led by her relatives and friends toward the church, where the groom in a hood, an acolyte, and a priest await her at the door. Two youths with a pipe and a portable organ play a tune. The scene bears no relation to the text above. See Montague Rhodes James, *Romance of Alexander* (Oxford, 1933), p. 32.

115. A Priest Receiving Tithes

A good man was ther of religioun,
And was a povre Persoun of a toun....
Ful looth were hym to cursen for his tithes.

General Prologue, 477f., 486

Miniature in MS British Museum Add, 20787, fol. 106v. Code of Laws drawn up by Alfonso X, King of Castile, called *Las Partidas.* Farmers bring grain and lambs to a priest as tithes.

116. A Plowman

With hym ther was a Plowman, was his brother.

General Prologue, 529

Miniature in Luttrell Psalter, British Museum Add. 42130, fol. 124. East Anglian manuscript, dated ca. 1340. See E. G. Millar, *Luttrell Psalter* (London, 1932), p. 43.

115

116

117. A Tally

> A gentil Maunciple was ther of a temple,
> Of which achatours myghte take exemple
> For to be wise in byynge of vitaille,
> For wheither that he payde or took by taille,
> Algate he wayted so in his achaat
> That he was ay biforn and in good staat.
>
> General Prologue, 567–71

The tally was a rod on which a debt was recorded by notches, and, when it was split, the creditor and the debtor each kept a half. The illustration shows a tally for 6s. 8d. (a noble, one-third of a pound), issued by the Treasurer of Edward I to the Sheriff of Lincolnshire. See on tallies H. Jenkinson in *Archaeologia*, LXXIV (1923–1924), 289–351.

THE KNIGHT'S TALE

119. The Same Death to Man and Beast

> "For slayn is man right as another beest."
>
> Knight's Tale, 1309

A page in MS Bibl. Nat. fr. 20029, fol. 6v. Deschamps's works. Date 1363. The rubric above the miniature reads: "Comment une fins et une mors est aussy bien aux homme come aux bestes." ("How one end and one death is for men as well as for beasts.") Below at the left is Deschamps's poem, and on the right is the passage from Pope Innocent III's *De Contemptu Mundi,* on which the poem is based. Chaucer translated several passages from Innocent and used them in the Man of Law's Prologue and Tale.

118

118. A Pardon

> His walet lay biforn hym in his lappe,
> Bretful of pardoun, comen from Rome al hoot.
>
> General Prologue (Pardoner), 686f.

Marginal sketch in MS Bodleian Library, Douce 104, fol. 44v. *Piers Plowman,* fifteenth century. A priest holds up a pardon with seal attached.

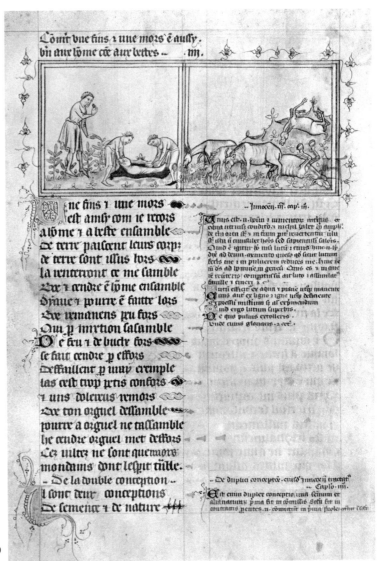

120. Venus, Cupid, and the Three Graces

The statue of Venus, glorious for to se,
Was naked, fletynge in the large see,
And fro the navele doun al covered was
With wawes grene, and brighte as any glas....
Above hir heed hir dowves flikerynge.
Biforn hire stood hir sone Cupido;
Upon his shuldres wynges hadde he two,
And blynd he was, as it is often seene;
A bowe he bar and arwes brighte and kene.

Knight's Tale, 1955–58, 1962–66

Miniature in MS Bibl. Nat. fr. 373, fol. 207v. *Ovide Moralisé,* which belonged to Jean Duc de Berry, bibliophile and patron of the arts. Date ca. 1400. The goose which Venus is grasping by the neck is due to a misreading of Latin *concam* (conch-shell) as *aucam* (goose). See E. Panofsky, *Renaissance and Renascences* (Stockholm, 1960), pp. 86f.; E. H. Wilkins in *Speculum,* XXXII (1957), 520f.

120

121, 122. Puella and Rubeus

And over his heed ther shynen two figures
Of sterres, that been cleped in scriptures,
That oon Puella, that oother Rubeus.

Knight's Tale, 2043–45

Miniatures in MS Bodleian Library, Bodley 581, fols. 19v, 20v. A treatise on geomancy composed for King Richard II in 1391, explaining a method of divination by means of dots set down at random. To each of the sixteen possible arrangements were assigned a name, a planet, and a sign of the zodiac. Under the word *Nomen* at the left we have the arrangement of dots called Puella, which was assigned to the planet Mars and the sign Libra. On the right at the top we have the arrangement

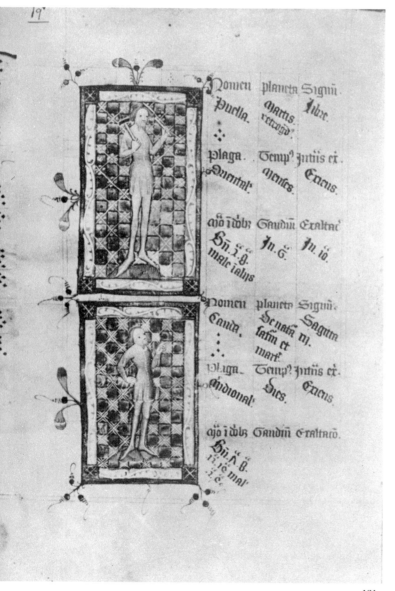

121

Rubeus, planet Mars, sign Gemini. Thus, because both Puella and Rubeus were supposed to indicate the influence of Mars, stars arranged in these two patterns were painted in his temple. The human figures represented in the miniatures seem to bear little relation to their names, Puella being depicted as a man with a hammer, and Rubeus as a man with a dagger. For a full explanation see Skeat in *Academy,* March 2, 1889.

123. *Alaunts*

Aboute his [Lygurge's] chaar ther wenten white
    alauntz,
Twenty and mo, as greet as any steer,
To hunten at the leoun or the deer,
And folwed hym with mosel faste ybounde,
Colered of gold, and tourettes fyled rounde.

Knight's Tale, 2148–52

A page in MS Bibl. Nat. fr. 619, fol. 33v. *Livre de la Chasse* by Gaston Phébus. Date end of fourteenth century. Wolf hounds and their cubs, with muzzles and collars as described by Chaucer, are fully treated by A. S. Cook in *Transactions of the Connecticut Academy of Arts and Sciences,* XXI (1916), 128–40.

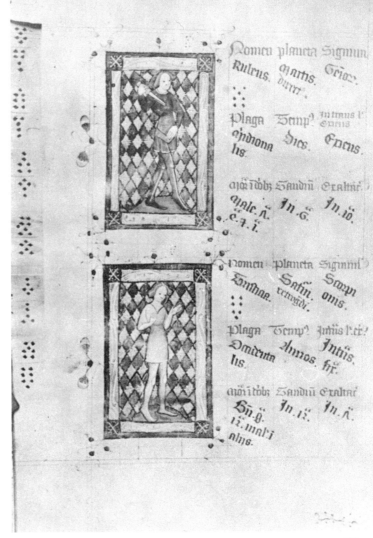

122

123

124

124. Diana

And therwithal Dyane gan appeere,
With bowe in honde, right as an hunteresse.

Knight's Tale, 2346f.

Miniature in MS Bibl. Nat. fr. 373, fol. 149. *Ovide Moralisé*. Date ca. 1400.

125. Knights Jousting

In goon the speres ful sadly in arrest;
In gooth the sharpe spore into the syde.

Knight's Tale, 2602f.

Drawing in a Lombard Sketchbook, Morgan Library, fol. 4. Date ca. 1350. Knights with crested helms, wearing *gypons,* spur at each other with leveled spears.

125

126. A Tournament

Ther seen men who kan juste and who kan ryde;
Ther shyveren shaftes upon sheeldes thikke; . . .
Out goon the swerdes as the silver brighte; . . .
Ther stomblen steedes stronge, and doun gooth al.

Knight's Tale, 2604–13

Miniature in MS British Museum Add. 12228, fols. 187v, 188. *Palamedes,* illuminated in Naples for King Louis of Taranto. Date 1352–1362. A tournament in which King Meliadus, King Mark, and the Good Knight without Fear participate. See

R. S. and L. H. Loomis, *Arthurian Legends in Medieval Art,* pp. 114f. Observe the wooden stand for the spectators and the various distinguishing helmet crests worn by some of the participants. In 1390 Chaucer was twice commissioned to oversee the erection of stands for tournaments in Smithfield outside the walls of London. For an account of the second tournament see E. Rickert, *Chaucer's World* (New York, 1948), pp. 211–14.

127. The Four Elements

"The Firste Moevere of the cause above,
Whan he first made the faire cheyne of love,
Greet was th'effect, and heigh was his entente, . . .
For with that faire cheyne of love he bond
The fyr, the eyr, the water and the lond
In certeyn boundes, that they may nat flee."

Knight's Tale, 2987–94

Miniature in MS Brussels Bibl. Royale 9094, fol. 45. *Propriétés des Choses.* The wavy lines below represent water; above to the left are flames of fire; a human corpse lies on the earth; above is a bank of cloud representing the air. Medieval science derived the notion of these four basic elements ultimately from the Greek Empedocles.

127

THE MILLER'S TALE

128. The East Window of St. Paul's Cathedral

Now was ther of that chirche a parissh clerk. . . .
With Poules wyndow corven on his shoos,
In hoses rede he wente fetisly.

                          Miller's Tale, 3312, 3318f.

Absalon, the dandified parish clerk of Oxford, wore shoes with the uppers cut in a pattern resembling the tracery of a window of St. Paul's Cathedral, permitting the scarlet hose to show beneath. See F. W. Fairholt, *Costume in England* (3rd ed.; London, 1885), II, 64f., and the shoes on one of the magi in Fig. 13. On this window see G. H. Cook, *Old St. Paul's Cathedral* (London, 1955), p. 36; pl. 11.

THE REEVE'S TALE

129. The Cross of Bromholm

"Help! hooly croys of Bromeholm," she seyde.

Reeve's Tale, 4286

Miniature in MS Fitzwilliam Museum, Cambridge, 55, fol. 57v. Book of Hours, date 1480. See *Journal of the Warburg Institute*, I (1937–38), 31–45. The cross here depicted differs from the norm by the addition of a second crossbar, as in the cross of Lorraine. It presumably contained what was alleged to be a piece of the true cross, brought from the East to Bromholm, Norfolk, in 1223, the goal of a very popular pilgrimage. See R. A. Pratt in *Modern Language Notes*, LXX (1955), 324f. The top and bottom of the rectangular frame of the miniature contain the Latin prayer: "Jesus nazarenus rex iudeorum Fili dei miserere mei." ("O Jesus of Nazareth, King of the Jews, Son of God, have mercy on me!") The right and left sides read: "Thys cros that here peyntyd is Syng [sign] of the cros of Bromholm is." A long rimed Latin prayer fills the space around the cross.

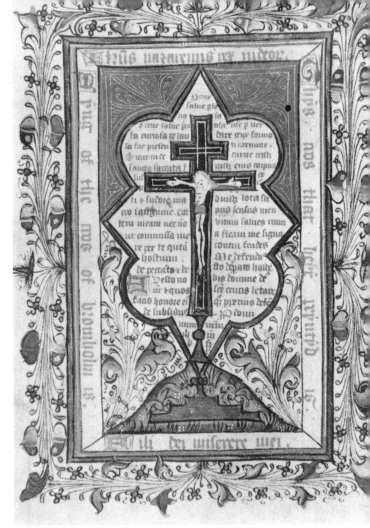

129

THE SHIPMAN'S TALE

130. The Punishment of Ganelon

"And but I do, God take on me vengeance
As foul as evere hadde Genylon of France."

Shipman's Tale, 193f.

O newe Scariot, newe Genylon!

Nun's Priest's Tale, 3227

Or the false Genelloun,
He that purchased the tresoun
Of Rowland and of Olyver.

Book of the Duchess, 1121–23

Miniature in MS Bibl. Nat. fr. 2813, fol. 124. *Chroniques de France*, date ca. 1379. According to the *Chanson de Roland* and later French pseudo-historical texts, Ganelon was the traitor who brought about the destruction of Charlemagne's rearguard and the death of Roland and Oliver in the pass of Roncevall, and who was punished by being torn to pieces by horses.

130

131. The Burning Bush a Type of the Virgin Mother

O mooder Mayde! o mayde Mooder free!
O bussh unbrent, brennynge in Moyses sighte,
That ravyshedest doun fro the Deitee,
Thurgh thyn humblesse, the Goost that in
th'alighte.

Prioress's Prologue, 467–70

Miniature in MS Bibl. Nat. lat. 9584, fol. 17v. A
Florentine copy of the *Speculum Humanae Salvationis*,
dated ca. 1390. On this manuscript see edition by
M. R. James and B. Berenson (Oxford, 1926),

and on the subject see E. Harris in *Journal of the
Courtauld Institute*, I (1937–1938), 281–86. It was a
commonplace of medieval thought that events in
the New Testament were prefigured in the Old.
Thus the bush burning in Moses' sight, yet un-
consumed, prefigured the Mother of Christ, im-
pregnated by the Holy Ghost (here represented
as a dove) yet remaining a virgin. The rubrics
read: "Maria concepit filium intacta et incorrupta.
Deus apparuit moysy in rubo." ("Mary conceived
a son, though untouched and undefiled. God ap-
peared to Moses in the bush.")

132

132. The Miracle of the Boy Singer

Miniature from MS Bodleian Library, Eng. poet. a. 1, fol. 124. English manuscript dated ca. 1380, which contains an analogue of the Prioress's Tale, printed in *Sources and Analogues of the "Canterbury Tales,"* ed. W. F. Bryan and G. Dempster, pp. 470–74. At upper right a Jew beckons the boy into his house; next left, he cuts the boy's throat; next left, he throws the corpse into a privy; at lower right, the boy's mother appeals to the mayor; at lower left, the corpse on the bier sings, "Salve, sancta parens" ("Hail, holy Mother"), while the bishop, having removed a lily from the boy's throat, begins to chant, "Requiem eternam [dona eis, Domine]" ("Grant them eternal rest, Lord").

SIR THOPAS

133. A *Symphonye*

> With harpe and pipe and symphonye.
>
> *Sir Thopas,* 815

Miniature in the Luttrell Psalter, British Museum Add. 42130, fol. 176. East Anglian manuscript, dated ca. 1340. A deformed minstrel is playing a *symphonye,* the original of the modern hurdy-gurdy. With one hand he turns a resined wheel which causes the strings to vibrate, and with the other he operates the stops.

133

134. A *Mazelyn*, or Mazer

They fette hym first the sweete wyn,
And mede eek in a mazelyn.

Sir Thopas, 851f.

A maple-wood bowl of the first half of the four-teenth century, preserved at Harbledown Hospital, near Canterbury. See *Archaeologia,* L (1887), part 1, pp. 139–42.

135. Sir Bevis of Hampton

Men speken of romances of prys,
Of Horn child and of Ypotys,
Of Beves and sir Gy.

Sir Thopas, 897–99

134

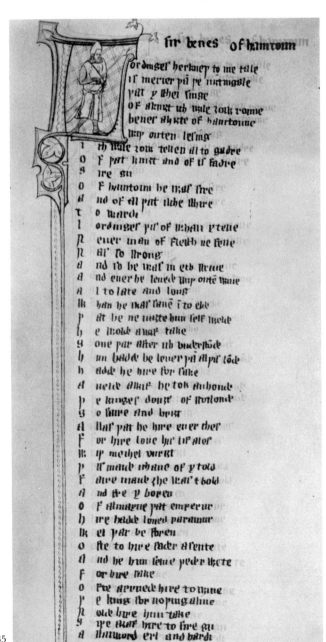

The Auchinleck MS National Library of Scotland, Adv. 19. 2. 1, fol. 176. A miscellaneous collection of popular verse, made in London ca. 1330. Chaucer was inspired by the somewhat crude romances in this very volume to write his parody, *Sir Thopas.* The opening lines of *Sir Bevis,* "Lord-inges, herkneth to me tale, is merier than the nightingale. . . . Of a knight ich wile yow roune," are echoed in lines 833–35 of *Sir Thopas:* "Yet listeth, lordes, to my tale Murier than the night-yngale, For now I wol yow rowne." See L. H. Loomis, *Adventures in the Middle Ages* (New York, 1962), pp. 150–87; *Sources and Analogues of the "Canterbury Tales,"* ed. W. F. Bryan, G. Dempster, pp. 489, 498.

136

136. Sir Guy of Warwick

Men speken of romances of prys, . . .
Of Beves and Sir Gy.

Sir Thopas, 897, 899

A silver gilt medallion set in the bottom of a mazer bowl at Harbledown Hospital, near Can-

135

terbury. Date first half of the fourteenth century. Inscription: "GY DE WARWYC: AD A NOUN: KE CI OCCIS: LE DRAGOUN:" ("He who here slays the dragon has Guy of Warwick for his name.") The knight is shown driving his spear into the reptile, thus releasing a grateful lion from its clutches—an incident in the very popular Anglo-Norman romance. The arms on Guy's shield (a fess between six crosslets) are appropriately those of the Beauchamp family, Earls of Warwick, who claimed descent from the legendary Guy. On the bowl and medallion see *Archaeologia*, L (1887), part 1, pp. 139–42. Sir William de Beauchamp, brother of the Earl of Warwick, was a friend of Chaucer's.

MELIBEUS

137. The Attack on Melibeus' Wife and Daughter

His wyf and eek his doghter hath he left inwith his hous, of which the dores weren faste yshette. Thre of his olde foes han it

espyed, and setten laddres to the walles of his hous, ... and betten his wyf and wounded his doghter.

Melibeus, 969–71

Miniature in MS Bibl. Nat. fr. 1165, fol. 66. Renaud de Louens, *Livre de Melibée et de Dame Prudence*, dated 1380–1390. The French text was Chaucer's source.

137

138. Job and His Three Friends

Remembre yow upon the pacient Job.

Melibeus, 998

Illustration from MS British Museum Royal 19. D. ii, fol. 195v. Bible in French, dated ca. 1350. Belonged to King John of France, was included in the booty taken by the English at the battle of Poitiers (1356), and was bought by William Montague, Earl of Salisbury, an acquaintance of Chaucer's, and given to his Countess Elizabeth. See *Catalogue of Western Manuscripts in the Royal and King's Collections*, ed. G. F. Warner and J. P. Gilson, II (London, 1921), 341f.

138

THE MONK'S TALE

139. The Fall of Nebuchadnezzar

This kyng of kynges proud was and elaat;
He wende that God, that sit in magestee,
Ne myghte hym nat bireve of his estaat.
But sodeynly he lost his dignytee,
And lyk a beest hym semed for to bee,
And eet hey as an oxe, and lay theroute
In reyn; with wilde beestes walked hee.

Monk's Tale, 2167–73

Page from MS Bibl. Nat. lat. 18014, fol. 9v. A collection of religious works made in 1390 for Louis II, Duc d'Anjou, nephew of King John and claimant to the throne of Sicily. Above we see Christ in majesty, holding a globe signifying dominion, and attended by angels. In the middle a Dominican friar admonishes a noble and points down to Nebuchadnezzar, naked, on all fours, surrounded by swine, a goat, and an ox.

140. Zenobia, Warrior and Huntress

Cenobia, of Palymerie queene, . . .
So worthy was in armes and so keene,
That no wight passed hire in hardynesse . . .
And many a wilde hertes blood she shedde
With arwes brode that she to hem sente.

Monk's Tale, 2247, 2249f., 2257f.

Miniature in MS Bibl. Nat. fr. 12420, fol. 152v. French translation of Boccaccio's *De Claris Mulieribus*. Date 1401. Zenobia is depicted on the right with bow and quiver of arrows, against a background of forest and wild animals; on the left she is presented with a helm and sword.

140

141. The Decapitation of Petro, King of Spain

O noble, O worthy Petro, glorie of Spayne, . . .
Out of thy land thy brother made thee flee. . . .
Thou were bitraysed and lad unto his tente,
Where as he with his owene hand slow thee,
Succedynge in thy regne and in thy rente.

Monk's Tale, 2375–82

Miniature in a *Life of Duguesclin* by Cuvelier, formerly owned by H. Y. Thompson. Date ca. 1390.

Petro's bastard brother, Henry of Trastamare, sits in a tent, having already stabbed Petro to death in a hand-to-hand struggle. A squire, who has cut off Petro's head, presents it to Henry. See H. Y. Thompson, *Illustrations from the Life of Bertrand Duguesclin* (London, 1909), pl. xii; H. L. Savage, "Chaucer and the 'Pitous Deeth' of 'Petro, Glorie of Spayne,'" *Speculum*, XXIV (1949), 357–75.

141

143. A Horologe at Wells Cathedral

A yeerd she hadde, enclosed al aboute
With stikkes, and a drye dych withoute,
In which she hadde a cok, hight Chauntecleer. . . .
Wel sikerer was his crowyng in his logge
Than is a clokke or an abbey orlogge.

Nun's Priest's Tale, 2847–54

In the north transept of Wells Cathedral is a clock made before 1392. At the top are figures of knights, which charge at each other every hour. In the corners of the square frame, angels hold heads representing the four winds. The outer circle is divided into twenty-four parts; an indicator representing the sun records the hours, while other indicators record the days of the lunar month and the minutes. See G. Sarton, *Introduction to the History of Science* (Baltimore, 1948), III, 1545; *Archaeologia*, LXXVII (1927), 257–74, 289–95.

142

142. Seneca

This Seneca, of which that I devyse,
By cause Nero hadde of hym swich drede, . . .
"Sire," wolde he seyn, "an emperour moot nede
Be vertuous and hate tirannye,"
For which he in a bath made hym to blede
On bothe his armes, til he moste dye.

Monk's Tale, 2503–10

Miniature in MS Brussels Bibl. Royale 9091, fol. 1. A French translation of the letters of Seneca. Date about 1390. In the upper left Seneca is writing in a book; in the upper right a messenger brings him a letter; in the lower left Nero kneels before him; in the lower right Nero sits on a throne while Seneca bleeds to death in a bathtub.

144. Cato Instructing His Son

"Lo Catoun, which that was so wys a man,
Seyde he nat thus, 'Ne do no fors of dremes'?"
Nun's Priest's Tale, 2940f.

Miniature in MS Bibl. Nat. fr. 1165, fol. 94. A French translation by Jean le Fevre of the *Distychs* of Dionysius Cato. The manuscript belonged to Jeanne, Duchess of Bourbon and Auvergne. Date 1380–1390. See R. Hazelton, "Chaucer and Cato," *Speculum,* XXXV (1960), 357.

145. Torture by Rack

"And right anon, ministres of that toun
Han hent the carter and so soore hym pyned
And eek the hostiler so soore engyned,
That they biknewe hire wikkednesse anon."
Nun's Priest's Tale, 3058–61

Miniature in MS British Museum Add. 15245, fol. 261v. Augustine, *City of God,* Book XIX. Date late fourteenth century.

144

Miniature in MS Bibl. de l'Arsénal, Paris, 5193, fol. 76v. A French translation of Boccaccio's *De Casibus Virorum Illustrium.* Date 1409–1419. A drowned man appears in a dream to warn Simonides not to take ship. See H. Martin, *Le Boccace de Jean sans Peur* (Brussels, 1911), pl. IX, fig. xxxiv.

145

146. The Warning Ghost

"That oon of hem, in slepyng as he lay,
Hym mette a wonder dreem agayn the day.
Hym thoughte a man stood by his beddes syde,
And hym comanded that he sholde abyde,
And seyde hym thus: 'If thou tomorwe wende,
Thow shalt be dreynt: my tale is at an ende.'"
Nun's Priest's Tale, 3077–82

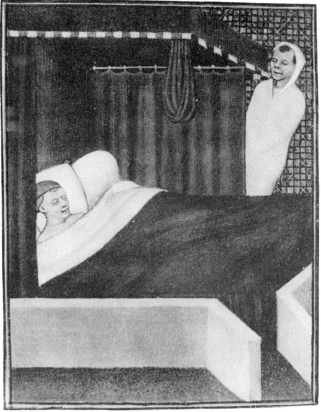

146

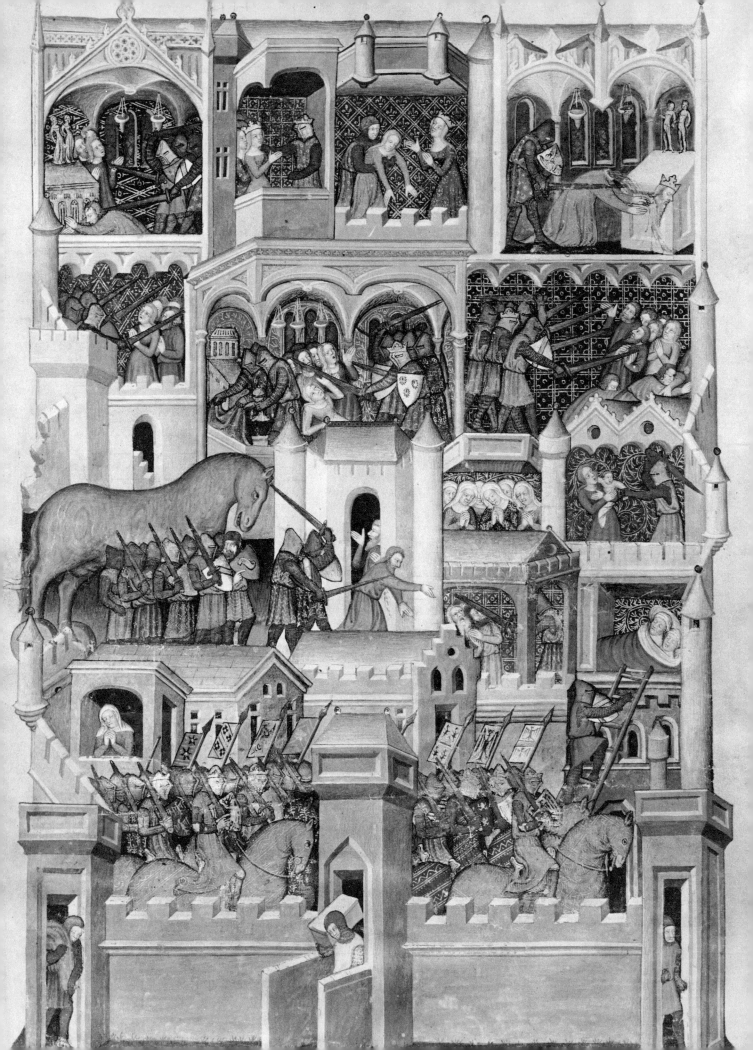

147. The Fall of Troy

Certes, swich cry ne lamentacion
Was nevere of ladyes maad whan Ylion
Was wonne, and Pirrus with his streite swerd,
Whan he hadde hent kyng Priam by the berd,
And slayn hym, as seith us *Eneydos*,
As maden alle the hennes in the clos.

Nun's Priest's Tale, 3355–60

Or elles it was the Grekes hors Synon,
That broghte Troie to destruccion,
As men moun in this olde geestes rede.

Squire's Tale, 209–11

Miniature in MS Bibl. Nat. fr. 301, fol. 147. *La Fleur des Histoires*. Date ca. 1390. The famous wooden horse is easily recognized. In the upper right corner Pyrrhus strikes off the head of Priam before an altar, on which are two nude images of gods. The mail armor, the long surcoats, and the helms seem to have been copied from a miniature of about the same date as that of *Bevis* in the Auchinleck manuscript, ca. 1330. See Fig. 135.

148. A Henwife Chases a Fox

This sely wydwe and eek hir doghtres two
Herden thise hennes crie and maken wo,
And out at dores stirten they anon,
And syen the fox toward the grove gon,
And bar upon his bak the cok away.

Nun's Priest's Tale, 3375–9

Marginal miniature in MS British Museum Stowe 17, fol. 209v, 210. Book of Hours, Flemish. Date 1300–1325. The marginal scene, including the boy in the tree picking pears, is totally irrelevant to the text, as was quite common in manuscript decoration of the period. See Figs. 104, 107, 108, 114, 116, 167, 173.

149

THE WIFE OF BATH'S PROLOGUE

149. The *Parables of Solomon*

> He hadde a book that gladly, nyght and day,
> For his desport he wolde rede alway....
> In which book eek ther was Tertulan, ...
> And eek the Parables of Salomon.
>
> Wife of Bath's Prologue, 669–79

Miniature in MS Bibl. de l'Arsénal, Paris, 5058, fol. 1. Translation by Guyart de Moulins of Comestor's *Bible,* which belonged to Jean Duc de Berry. Date ca. 1410. Above left, Solomon judging between two women who claim a child; below left, Solomon teaching young scholars. Above right, the death of Adonias; below right, Solomon receiving the Queen of Sheba. On the subjects of the miniature see *Catalogue of Western Manuscripts in the Old Royal and King's Collections,* ed. G. F. Warner, J. P. Gilson, II (1921), 261, 342.

THE SUMMONER'S TALE

150. A Friar Preaching

> And so bifel that on a day this frere
> Hadde preched at a chirche in his manere.
>
> Summoner's Tale, 1713f.

A miniature in a MS of the *Canterbury Tales,* Bodleian Library, Rawlinson poet. 223, fol. 142. Initial at the beginning of the Friar's Prologue. Date ca. 1450. A Franciscan friar is depicted standing in a pulpit, holding an aspergill, or holy-water sprinkler, in his right hand. See *Text of the "Canterbury Tales,"* ed. Manly and Rickert, I, 464, 583, 590f. On friars see "The 'Limitour' of Chaucer's Time and His 'Limitacioun,'" *Studies in Philology,* LVII (1960), 463–78.

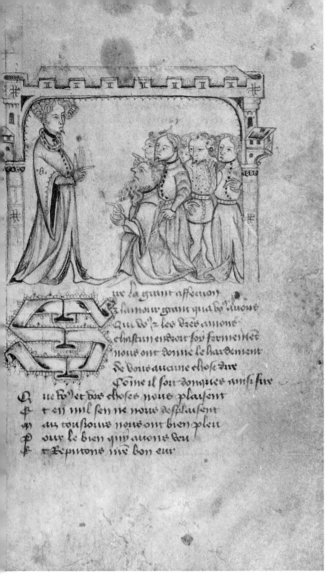

151

151. The Marquis Is Advised to Wed

> . . . He nolde—and that was worst of alle—
> Wedde no wyf, for noght that may bifalle.
> Oonly that point his peple bar so soore
> That flokmeele on a day they to hym wente,
> And oon of hem, that wisest was of loore . . .
> He to the markys seyde as ye shul heere.
>
> Clerk's Tale, 83–87, 91. MS fol. 7

152. The Marquis Hunts a Stag

> . . . On his lust present was al his thoght,
> As for to hauke and hunte on every syde.
>
> Clerk's Tale, 80f. MS fol. 14

152

THE CLERK'S TALE
OF GRISILD

The tale of Grisild (or Griselda) is amply illustrated
by the drawings in the manuscript of a play on
the subject, Bibl. Nat. fr. 2203, dated 1395. En-
titled *L'Estoire* [Drama] *de Griseldis,* it is based on
a French prose translation by Philippe de Mézières,
counsellor of Charles VI of France, from Petrarch's
Latin version of Boccaccio's story in the *Decameron.*
Thus Petrarch's text was the indirect source of
these French drawings and was also one of the
indirect sources of Chaucer's poem, composed
only a few years before the drawings were made.
The *Estoire de Griseldis* was edited by Mario
Roques (Geneva, Paris, 1957), with a full description of the drawings.

153. Grisild and Her Father

Amonges thise povre folk ther dwelte a man
Which that was holden povrest of hem alle....
A doghter hadde he, fair ynogh to sighte,
And Grisildis this yonge mayden highte.

Clerk's Tale, 204f., 209f. MS fol. 15v.

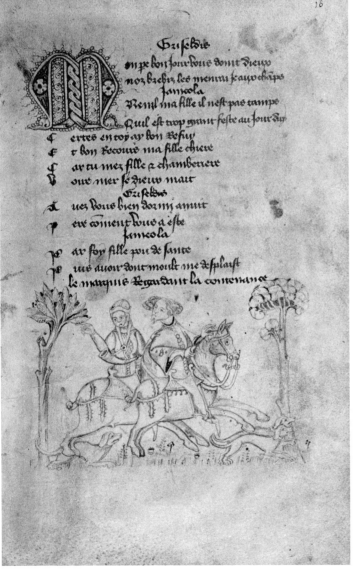

154. The Marquis Observes Grisild

Upon Grisilde, this povre creature,
Ful ofte sithe this markys sette his ÿe
As he on huntyng rood paraventure.

Clerk's Tale, 232–34. MS fol. 16

155. The Marquis Calls Grisild

Grisilde of this, God woot, ful innocent, . . .
To fecchen water at a welle is went. . . .
The markys cam, and gan hire for to calle;
And she set doun hir water pot anon.

    Clerk's Tale, 274, 276, 289f. MS fol. 20

156. The Marquis Announces His Choice of Grisild

"This is ynogh, Grisilde myn," quod he,
And forth he gooth, with a full sobre cheere, . . .
And to the peple he seyde in this manere:
"This is my wyf," quod he, "that standeth heere.
Honoureth hire and loveth hire, I preye."

    Clerk's Tale, 365f., 368–70. MS fol. 22v.

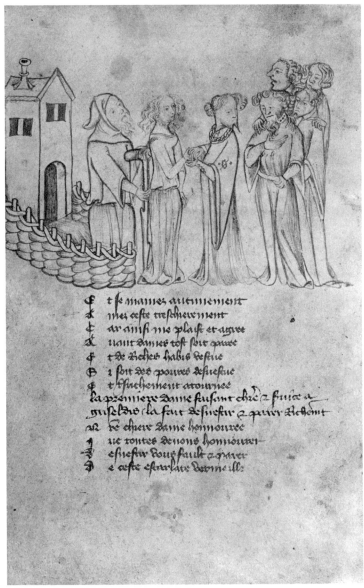

157. Grisild Gives Birth to a Girl

Nat longe tyme after that this Grisild
Was wedded, she a doghter hath ybore....
Glad was this markys and the folk therfore.

Clerk's Tale, 442f., 445. MS fol. 28v.

158. Grisild Signs Her Daughter
with the Cross

And whan this sergeant wiste his lordes wille,
Into the chambre he stalked hym ful stille.
"Madame," he seyde, "ye moote foryeve it me....
This childe I am comanded for to take." ...
And thus she seyde in hire benigne voys,
"Fareweel my child! I shal thee nevere see."

Clerk's Tale, 524–26, 533, 554f. MS fol. 31

159. Grisild Gives Her Robe Back to the Marquis

"... Heere agayn your clothyng I restoore."
Clerk's Tale, 867. MS fol. 46v.

160. The Marquis Bids Grisild Prepare for a Successor

"I have no wommen suffisaunt, certayn,
The chambres for t'arraye in ordinaunce
After my lust, and therfore wolde I fayn
That thyn were al swich manere governaunce."
Clerk's Tale, 960–63. MS fol. 50

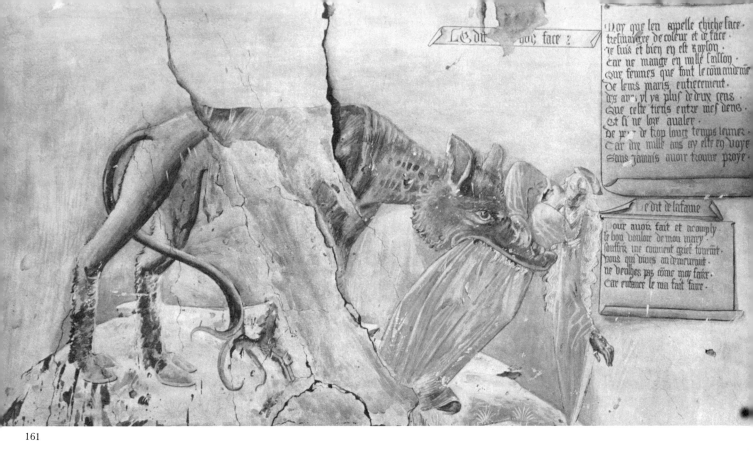

161

161, 162. Chicheface and Bigorne

O noble wyves, ful of heigh prudence,
Lat noon humylitee youre tonge naille . . .
Lest Chichevache yow swelwe in hire entraille!

Clerk's Tale, 1183f., 1188

A mural painting (late fifteenth century) in the castle of Villeneuve-Lembron (Puy-de-Dôme), representing a fabulous beast which fed only on obedient wives, nearly starved because of their scarcity, and was called Chicheface, Lean-Face. A variant on the name, Chichevache, Lean-Cow, was used by Chaucer. See on the subject Eleanor Hammond, *English Verse between Chaucer and Surrey* (Durham, N. C., 1927), pp. 113f. Another painting at the same castle depicts the contrasting figure of a monster named Bigorne, which subsisted on obedient husbands and because of abundant supply waxed very fat.

162

THE SQUIRE'S TALE

163. A Birthday Feast of the Great Khan

And so bifel that whan this Cambyuskan
Hath twenty wynter born his diademe,
As he was wont fro yeer to yeer, I deme,
He leet the feeste of his nativitee
Doon cryen thurghout Sarray his citee.

Squire's Tale, 42–46

Miniature in MS Bodleian Library, Bodley 264, fol. 239. Illustrates Marco Polo's *Travels,* English workmanship, ca. 1410. Rubric: "Cy devise li iiii^{xx} et vi chapitre de la grant feste que le grant caan fait chascun an de sa nati[vité]." ("Here the 86th chapter tells of the great birthday feast which the Great Khan makes every year.") In the foreground is a fountain, flowing with wine. The Khan sits under a canopy, holding a precious goblet, and other goblets adorn the tables. Four crowned ladies, his wives, sit in niches (*tabernacles*), while in the upper corners "mynstralles hir thynges pleye." For another feast scene see Fig. 41.

163

164. Minstrels

They sownen diverse instrumentz,
That it is lyk an hevene for to heere.

Squire's Tale, 270f.

Miniature in MS Bodleian Library, Bodley 264, fol. 188v. French *Alexander,* made at Bruges, date 1338–1344. The rubric has no connection with the miniature. Beginning at the left, the minstrels play *cornemuse* (bagpipe), drum, *nakers* (kettle-drums), cymbals, bells, double trumpet, *fithele,* portative organ, *sautrye* (psaltery), and *giterne.* On minstrels and music in Chaucer see C. C. Olson in *Speculum,* XVII (1941), 64–91, and F. Montgomery in *Musical Quarterly,* XVII (1931), 439–48. For other musical instruments see Figs. 43, 61, 72, 96, 114.

164

THE FRANKLIN'S TALE

165. A Banquet Accompanied by a Pantomimic Siege

"For ofte at feestes have I wel herd seye
That tregetours, withinne an halle large,
Have maad come in a water and a barge, . . .
Somtyme a castel, al of lym and stoon;
And whan hem lyked, voyded it anon."

Franklin's Tale, 1142–44, 1149f.

Miniature in ms Bibl. Nat. fr. 2813, fol. 473v. *Chroniques de France,* date ca. 1379. On January 6, 1378, Charles V of France entertained the Emperor Charles IV and his son Wenceslas in the royal palace, Paris, with a pantomime representing the arrival of the Crusaders and the capture of Jerusalem in 1099. Godfrey de Bouillon (distinguished by the crosses on his shield and *gypon*) is followed, anachronistically, up the scaling ladder by Richard

Lion Heart (distinguished similarly by the leopards of England). In the barge stands Peter the Hermit, who preached the First Crusade. Probably Chaucer had heard of this spectacle—the introduction of water, a barge, and a castle into a great hall during a feast—and referred in the lines above to the designers and operators of these stage properties as magicians, "tregetours." See *Speculum,* XXXIII (1958), 242–48; reprinted in L. H. Loomis, *Adventures in the Middle Ages* (New York, 1962), pp. 274–81.

THE PHYSICIAN'S TALE

166. Virginius Slays Virginia

And with that word she preyed hym ful ofte
That with his swerd he wolde smyte softe. . . .
Hir fader, with ful sorweful herte and wil,
Hir heed of smoot.

Physician's Tale, 251f., 254f.

Miniature in ms Bibl. Nat. fr. 12420, fol. 90. French translation of Boccaccio's *De Claris Mulieribus.* Date 1401.

THE PARDONER'S HEADLINK AND TALE

167. Drinking at an Ale-Stake

> "It shal be doon," quod he, "by Seint Ronyon!
> But first," quod he, "heere at this ale-stake
> I wol bothe drynke and eten of a cake."
>
> Pardoner's Headlink, 320–22

Miniature (ca. 1325) in MS British Museum Royal 10 E iv, fol. 114v. The *Decretals* of Pope Gregory in Latin. Though the text was copied in Italy, the wholly irrelevant miniatures in the lower borders were done in England. This one depicts a hermit drinking in front of a tavern, from which an ale-stake projects. The tonsured apparition above the tavern is a characteristic piece of meaningless foolery. On such grotesques see *Metropolitan Museum of Art Bulletin,* June 1958.

167

168. The Sins of Swearing and Gambling

> Hir othes been so grete and so dampnable
> That it is grisly for to heere hem swere.
> Oure blissed Lordes body they totere.
>
> Pardoner's Tale, 472–74

> "By Goddes precious herte," and "By his nayles, . .
> By Goddes armes, if thou falsly pleye,
> This daggere shal thurghout thyn herte go."
>
> Pardoner's Tale, 651, 654f.

A mural painting (ca. 1430) at Broughton church, Buckinghamshire. The Virgin holds the mutilated body of Christ in her arms. Five men hold the various members by which they have sworn. See Lowes in *Romanic Review,* II (1911), 115–17. Below, three other men quarrel over a gambling game called "tables." On this painting see Mary D. Anderson, *Drama and Imagery in Medieval English Churches* (Cambridge, 1963), pp. 58f.

168

169. A *Tombestere* and Musicians

And right anon thanne comen tombesteres.
Pardoner's Tale, 477

Drawing in the Morgan Library, Lombard Sketch-book, fol. 13v. Date ca. 1350. A woman acrobat performing, while another woman strikes a tambourine and a man plays the pipe and tabor.

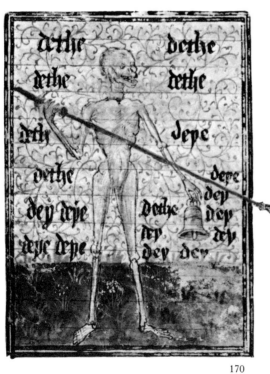

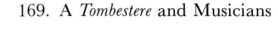

170

170. Death with His Spear

"Ther cam a privee theef men clepeth Deeth,
That in this contree al the peple sleeth,
And with his spere he smoot his herte atwo."
Pardoner's Tale, 675–77

Miniature in MS Bodleian Library Douce 322, fol. 19v. Illustrates Lydgate's *Death's Warning to the World*, ed. H. N. MacCracken, Early English Text Society, CXCII, p. 655.

Ӡn non essent regiltrantes que non viderunt nec sciunt:
et futuris ministrantes que per scripturas edocemur
vident et que audiunt. si nos bene recordemur. que sunt

171. The Black Death

"He [Deeth] hath a thousand slayn this pestilence."
Pardoner's Tale, 679

Miniature in MS Brussels, Bibl. Royale, 13076–77, fol. 24v. Dated ca. 1355. A rimed Latin chronicle of the events of 1349–1352 by Egidius, abbot of St. Martin's, Tournai. Depicted is the burial of victims of the plague of 1349.

172. An Apothecary's Shop

And forth he gooth, no lenger wolde he tarie,
Into the toun, unto a pothecarie.
Pardoner's Tale, 851f.

"By corpus bones! but I have triacle. . . ."
Pardoner's Headlink, 314

A miniature in MS Imperial Library, Vienna, 2617, dated ca. 1400. *Tacuinum Sanitatis,* a medical handbook made in Verona. The miniature illustrates *triacha,* Chaucer's *triacle,* and shows a customer, an apothecary, and his apprentice. See *Jahrbuch der kunsthistorischen Sammlungen des allerhöchsten Kaiserhauses,* XVI (1895), 144–214; pl. XVI,

fig. 1. On *triacle,* a salve used as an antidote against poison, see Muriel J. Hughes, *Women Healers in Medieval Life and Literature* (New York, 1943), pp. 27, 47f.

173

THE MANCIPLE'S PROLOGUE

173. Jousting at the Fan of a Quintain

"Now, sweete sire, wol ye justen atte fan?"
Manciple's Prologue, 42

Miniature in MS Bodleian Library, Bodley 264, fol. 82v. French *Alexander,* made at Bruges. Date 1338–1344. A youth is running with a lance, as in a joust, at a "fan," while another is holding up a bag of sand, which, if the runner does not dodge it, will fly round and hit his head or his back. See on the miniature M. R. James, *Romance of Alexander* (Oxford, 1933), p. 27; on the game see Strutt, *Sports and Pastimes,* ed. Hone (London, 1876), pp. 182ff.

174

THE SECOND NUN'S TALE

174. St. Cecilia and the Two Garlands

This angel hadde of roses and of lilie
Corones two, the which he bar in honde;
And first to Cecile as I understonde,
He yaf that oon, and after gan he take
That oother to Valerian, hir make.
Second Nun's Tale, 220–24

Detail from a painted rood screen in the church at North Elmham, Norfolk. Date late fifteenth century. Note the two garlands combining roses with lilies, red signifying the blood of martyrdom, and white virginity. On the symbolism see Tatlock in *Publications of the Modern Language Association,* XLV (1930), 169–79.

THE CANON'S
YEOMAN'S TALE

175. An Alchemist's Laboratory

> I blowe the fir til that myn herte feynte. . . .
> Ther is also ful many another thyng
> That is unto oure craft apertenyng . . .
> . . sondry vessels maad of erthe and glas,
> Oure urynales and oure descensories,
> Violes, crosletz, and sublymatories.
>
>   Canon's Yeoman's Tale, 753, 784f.,791–93

175

Detail of miniature in MS British Museum Add. 10302, fol. 37. Thomas Norton, *Ordinal of Alchemy,* date ca. 1500. Two yeomen, employed by an alchemist, are tending furnaces which "sublime," i.e., vaporize, solid substances in vessels called "sublimatories." The Latin inscriptions on the scrolls seem to have little bearing on the operation.

THE PARSON'S TALE

176. Dante and Virgil Witness the Torments of Hell

> Al the sorwe that a man myghte make fro the bigynnyng of the world nys but a litel thyng at regard of the sorwe of helle. . . . they shulle be naked in body as of clothyng . . . hire covertures shulle been of wormes of helle.
>
>   Parson's Tale, 179, 195, 197

A fifteenth-century wall painting in the church of San Giorgio di Campochiesa near Albenga. The larger part is taken up with the punishment by diligent devils of six of the seven sins: *superbia* (pride), *invidia* (envy), *acidia* (sloth), *gula* (gluttony), *avaricia* (avarice), and *luxuria* (lust). On the right is a spiked wheel operated by a devil, on which the damned are caught and plunged into a pit. At the left we see illustrated the famous passage in Dante's *Inferno,* canto xxxii, where the poet and his guide Virgil come upon Count Ugolino gnawing the nape of Archbishop Ruggieri, who had starved Ugolino and his sons to death in the Tower of Hunger at Pisa. Chaucer knew this passage well, since he retells Ugolino's story in the Monk's Tale.

176

177. Envy and Charity

Certes, thanne is love the medicine that casteth out the venym of Envye fro mannes herte.

Parson's Tale, 531

A manuscript of the *Canterbury Tales,* Cambridge University Library Gg. 4. 27, dated ca. 1450–1460, depicts some of the Virtues and Vices treated in the Parson's Tale. The miniatures are described from the technical angle by M. Rickert in *Text of the Canterbury Tales,* ed. J. M. Manly and E. Rickert (Chicago, 1940), I, 593–96. For other examples of Vices mounted on appropriate animals see A. Katzenellenbogen, *Allegories of Virtues and Vices in Mediaeval Art* (London, 1939), pp. 60f.; S. Chew, "Spenser's Pageant of the Seven Deadly Sins," *Studies in Art and Literature for Belle da Costa Greene,* ed. D. Miner (Princeton, N.J.), pp. 37–54; E. Mâle, *L'Art Religieux de la Fin du Moyen Age* (2nd ed.; Paris, 1922), pp. 328–34.

Miniature from fol. 416. Envy is personified as a man in a long-sleeved gown, with a dagger at his belt. He is riding a beast, presumably a wolf, holds in his right hand a leash attached to the beast's collar, and in his left a bone for the beast to gnaw. Charity, that is, Love, is represented by a woman in flowing robes, holding in one hand a scepter and in the other a flaming, winged heart. She is nimbed and wears a triple crown.

177

178. Gluttony and Abstinence

Agayns Glotonye is the remedie abstinence.

Parson's Tale, 831

Miniature from fol. 432. Gluttony is represented as a potbellied man, holding an entrail on which a kite feeds. He is mounted on a bear. Abstinence is personified as a woman in flowing robes, crowned and nimbed, holding a water pitcher in one hand and a vegetable in the other.

179. Lechery and Chastity

Now comth the remedie agayns Leccherie, and that is generally chastitee. . . .

Parson's Tale, 915

Miniature from fol. 433. Lechery is personified by a lady in fashionable costume, riding a he-goat, a sparrow perched on her finger, both animal and bird symbolizing lust. Chastity is personified by an excessively tall lady, wearing a mantle lined with ermine, trampling a monster representing the same vice. Her saintly character is indicated by a halo and by a cross-headed spear with which she transfixes the monster.

INDEX OF FIGURES

This index refers only to the subjects represented in the illustrations,
and does not cover all the topics mentioned in the text.